9th Web as Corpus Workshop

(WaC-9 2014)

Held at the 14th Conference of the European Chapter of the Association for Computational Linguistics

Gothenburg, Sweden
26 April 2014

ISBN: 978-1-63266-399-3

Printed from e-media with permission by:

Curran Associates, Inc.
57 Morehouse Lane
Red Hook, NY 12571

CURRAN ASSOCIATES INC. proceedings.com

Some format issues inherent in the e-media version may also appear in this print version.

Printed by Curran Associates, Inc. (2014)

Association for Computational Linguistics
209 N. Eighth Street
Stroudsburg, Pennsylvania 18360

Phone: 1-570-476-8006
Fax: 1-570-476-0860

acl@aclweb.org

Additional copies of this publication are available from:

Curran Associates, Inc.
57 Morehouse Lane
Red Hook, NY 12571 USA
Phone: 845-758-0400
Fax: 845-758-2634
Email: curran@proceedings.com
Web: www.proceedings.com

Preface

The World Wide Web has become increasingly popular as a source of linguistic data, not only within the NLP communities, but also with theoretical linguists facing problems of data sparseness or data diversity. Accordingly, web corpora continue to gain importance, given their size and diversity in terms of genres/text types. However, after a decade of activity in the web-as-corpus community, a number of issues in web corpus construction still needs much research.

For instance, questions concerning sampling strategies and their relation to crawling algorithms have not yet been explored in any detail so far. Virtually all existing large web corpora were sampled using breath-first web crawls, which demonstrably yield biased results and make the corpus particularly vulnerable to criticism targeting their sampling frame. In addition, relying on the results of commercial search engines when selecting the seed URLs for such crawls (as has been common practice) introduces an additional bias. This is also an issue for smaller web corpora obtained without web crawling, by simply downloading a number of documents fixed in advance.

Turning to the linguistic post-processing of web corpora, problems may arise, among other things, from the kind of non-copy edited, quasi-spontaneous language typical of numerous genres of computer-mediated communication. Spelling errors and deliberate non-standard spellings are a case in point, and grammatical variation as well as (semi-)graphical elements like emoticons also figure prominently. Technically, all of these present challenges for NLP tools (such as POS-taggers, parsers etc.) that expect "clean", copy-edited standard language. From a conceptual point of view, such variation begs the question whether (and to what extent) web corpora should be normalized and how this can be achieved in a transparent and non-destructive way.

A similar point can be made when it comes to document filtering: Currently available web corpora have usually undergone radical cleaning procedures in order to produce "high-quality" data. However, at least for some uses of the data, aggressive and sometimes arbitrary removal of material in the form of whole documents or parts thereof can be problematic.

Finally, the systematic evaluation of web corpora, for example in the form of task-based comparisons to traditional corpora, has only lately shifted into focus.

Against this backdrop, most of the contributions included in this volume address particular problems related to data collection and normalization, while others offer a broader perspective on the process of constructing a particular web corpus. The papers were selected after a highly competitive review process, and we would like to thank all those who submitted, as well as the program committee who contributed to the review process.

Felix Bildhauer & Roland Schäfer, March 2014

WaC-9 Program Chairs

Felix Bildhauer, Freie Universität Berlin (Germany)
Roland Schäfer, Freie Universität Berlin (Germany)

WaC-9 Program Committee

Adrien Barbaresi, École Normale Supérieure de Lyon (France)
Silvia Bernardini, Università di Bologna (Italy)
Chris Biemann, Technische Universität Darmstadt (Germany)
Jesse Egbert, Northern Arizona University (USA)
Stefan Evert, Friedrich-Alexander Universität Erlangen-Nürnberg (Germany)
Adriano Ferraresi, Università di Bologna (Italy)
William Fletcher, United States Naval Academy (USA)
Dirk Goldhahn, Universität Leipzig (Germany)
Adam Kilgarriff, Lexical Computing Ltd. (UK)
Anke Lüdeling, Humboldt-Universität Berlin (Germany)
Alexander Mehler, Goethe-Universität Frankfurt am Main (Germany)
Uwe Quasthoff, Universität Leipzig (Germany)
Paul Rayson, Lancaster University (UK)
Serge Sharoff, University of Leeds (UK)
Sabine Schulte im Walde, Universität Stuttgart (Germany)
Egon Stemle, European Academy of Bozen/Bolzano (Italy)
Yannick Versley, Universität Heidelberg (Germany)
Stephen Wattam, Lancaster University (UK)
Torsten Zesch, Universität Darmstadt (Germany)

Table of Contents

Conference Program

11:15-11:30 Welcome by Felix Bildhauer, Roland Schäfer

11:30–12:00 *Finding Viable Seed URLs for Web Corpora: A Scouting Approach and Comparative Study of Available Sources*
Adrien Barbaresi

12:00–12:30 *Focused Web Corpus Crawling*
Roland Schäfer, Adrien Barbaresi and Felix Bildhauer

14:00–14:30 *Less Destructive Cleaning of Web Documents by Using Standoff Annotation*
Maik Stührenberg

14:30–15:00 *Some Issues on the Normalization of a Corpus of Products Reviews in Portuguese*
Magali Sanches Duran, Lucas Avanço, Sandra Aluísio, Thiago Pardo and Maria da Graça Volpe Nunes

15:00–15:30 *bs,hr,srWaC - Web Corpora of Bosnian, Croatian and Serbian*
Nikola Ljubešić and Filip Klubička

16:00–16:30 *The PAISÀ Corpus of Italian Web Texts*
Verena Lyding, Egon Stemle, Claudia Borghetti, Marco Brunello, Sara Castagnoli, Felice Dell'Orletta, Henrik Dittmann, Alessandro Lenci and Vito Pirrelli

16:30–17:00 *Internet Data in a Study of Language Change and a Program Helping to Work with Them*
Varvara Magomedova, Natalia Slioussar and Maria Kholodilova

17:00-18:00 Discussion

Finding viable seed URLs for web corpora: a scouting approach and comparative study of available sources

Adrien Barbaresi
ICAR Lab
ENS Lyon & University of Lyon
15 parvis René Descartes, 69007 Lyon, France
adrien.barbaresi@ens-lyon.fr

Abstract

The conventional tools of the "web as corpus" framework rely heavily on URLs obtained from search engines. Recently, the corresponding querying process became much slower or impossible to perform on a low budget. I try to find acceptable substitutes, i.e. viable link sources for web corpus construction. To this end, I perform a study of possible alternatives, including social networks as well as the Open Directory Project and Wikipedia. Four different languages (Dutch, French, Indonesian and Swedish) taken as examples show that complementary approaches are needed. My scouting approach using open-source software leads to a URL directory enriched with metadata which may be used to start a web crawl. This is more than a drop-in replacement for existing tools since said metadata enables researchers to filter and select URLs that fit particular needs, as they are classified according to their language, their length and a few other indicators such as host- and markup-based data.

1 Introduction

1.1 The "web as corpus" paradigm and its URL seeds problem

The state of the art tools of the "web as corpus" framework rely heavily on URLs obtained from search engines. The BootCaT method (Baroni and Bernardini, 2004) consists in repeated search engine queries using several word seeds that are randomly combined, first coming from an initial list and later from unigram extraction over the corpus itself. As a result, so-called "seed URLs" are gathered which are used as a starting point for web crawlers. This approach is not limited to English: it has been successfully used by Baroni et al. (2009) and Kilgarriff et al. (2010) for major world languages.

Until recently, the BootCaT method could be used in free web corpus building approaches. To my best knowledge it is now passé because of increasing limitations on the search engines' APIs, which make the querying process on a low budget much slower or impossible. Other technical difficulties include diverse and partly unknown search biases due in part to search engine optimization tricks as well as undocumented PageRank adjustments. All in all, the APIs may be too expensive and/or too unstable to support large-scale corpus building projects.

API changes are combined with an evolving web document structure and a slow but inescapable shift from "web as corpus" to "web for corpus" due to the increasing number of web pages and the necessity of using sampling methods at some stage. This is what I call the post-BootCaT world in web corpus construction.[1]

Moreover, the question whether the method used so far, i.e. randomizing keywords, provides a good overview of a language is still open. It now seems reasonable to look for alternatives, so that research material does not depend on a single data source, as this kind of black box effect combined with paid queries really impedes reproducibility of research. Using diverse sources of URL seeds could at least ensure that there is not a single bias, but several.

Additionally, the lack of interest and project financing when dealing with certain less-resourced languages makes it necessary to use light-weight

[1] Note that the proponents of the BootCaT method seem to acknowledge this evolution, see for example Marco Baroni's talk at this year's BootCaTters of the world unite (BOTWU) workshop: "My love affair with the Web... and why it's over!"

approaches where costs are lowered as much as possible (Scannell, 2007). In this perspective, a preliminary light scouting approach and a full-fledged focused crawler like those used by the Spiderling (Suchomel and Pomikálek, 2012) or the COW (Schäfer and Bildhauer, 2012) projects are complementary. A "web for corpus" crawling method using a seed set enriched with metadata as described in this article may yield better results, e.g. ensure a more diverse and less skewed sample distribution in a population of web documents, and/or reach faster a given quantitative goal.

1.2 Looking for alternatives, what issues do we face?

Search engines have not been taken as a source simply because they were convenient. They actually yield good results in terms of linguistic quality. The main advantage was to outsource operations such as web crawling and website quality filtering, which are considered to be too costly or too complicated to deal with while the main purpose is actually to build a corpus.

In fact, it is not possible to start a web crawl from scratch, so the main issue to tackle can be put this way: where may we find web pages which are bound to be interesting for corpus linguists and which in turn contain many links to other interesting web pages?

Researchers in the machine translation field have started another attempt to outsource competence and computing power, making use of data gathered by the CommonCrawl project[2] to find parallel corpora (Smith et al., 2013). Nonetheless, the quality of the links may not live up to their expectations. First, purely URL-based approaches are a trade-off in favor of speed which sacrifices precision, and language identification tasks are a good example of this phenomenon (Baykan et al., 2008). Second, machine-translated content is a major issue, so is text quality in general, especially when it comes to web texts (Arase and Zhou, 2013). Third, mixed-language documents slow down text gathering processes (King and Abney, 2013). Fourth, link diversity is a also problem, which in my opinion has not got the attention it deserves. Last, the resource is constantly moving. There are not only fast URL changes and ubiquitous redirections. Following the "web 2.0" paradigm, much web content is being injected from other sources, so that many web pages are now expected to change any time.[3] Regular exploration and re-analysis could be the way to go to ensure the durability of the resource.

In the remainder of this paper, I introduce a scouting approach which considers the first issue, touches on the second one, provides tools and metrics to address the third and fourth, and adapts to the last. In the following section I describe my methodology, then I show in detail which metrics I decided to use, and last I discuss the results.

2 Method

2.1 Languages studied

I chose four different languages in order to see if my approach generalizes well: Dutch, French, Indonesian and Swedish. It enables me to compare several language-dependent web spaces which ought to have different if not incompatible characteristics. In fact, the "speaker to website quantity" ratio is probably extremely different when it comes to Swedish and Indonesian. I showed in a previous study that this affects greatly link discovery and corpus construction processes (Barbaresi, 2013a).

French is spoken on several continents and Dutch is spoken in several countries (Afrikaans was not part of this study). Indonesian offers an interesting point of comparison, as the chances to find web pages in this language during a crawl at random are scarce. For this very reason, I explicitly chose not to study English or Chinese because they are clearly the most prominently represented languages on the web.

2.2 Data sources

I use two reference points, the first one being the existing method depending on search engine queries, upon which I hope to cast a new light with this study. The comparison grounds on URLs retrieved using the BootCaT seed method on the meta-engine E-Tools[4] at the end of 2012. The second reference point consists of social networks, to whose linguistic structure I already dedicated a study (Barbaresi, 2013b) where the method used to find the URLs is described in detail. I chose to adopt a different perspective, to re-examine the URLs I gathered and to add relevant metadata

[2]http://commoncrawl.org/

[3]This is the reason why Marco Baroni states in the talk mentioned above that his "love affair with the web" is over.

[4]http://www.etools.ch/

in order to see how they compared to the other sources studied here.

I chose to focus on three different networks: FriendFeed, an aggregator that offers a broader spectrum of retrieved information; identi.ca, a microblogging service similar to Twitter; and Reddit, a social bookmarking and microblogging platform. Perhaps not surprisingly, these data sources display the issues linked to API instability mentioned above. The example of identi.ca is telling: until March 2013, when the API was closed after the company was bought, it was a social microblogging service built on open source tools and open standards, the advantages compared to Twitter include the Creative Commons license of the content, and the absence of limitations on the total number of pages seen.

Another data source is the Open Directory Project (DMOZ[5]), where a selection of links is curated according to their language and/or topic. The language classification is expected to be adequate, but the amount of viable links is an open question, as well as the content.

Last, the free encyclopedia Wikipedia is another spam-resilient data source in which the quality of links is expected to be high. It is acknowledged that the encyclopedia in a given language edition is a useful resource, the open question resides in the links pointing to the outside world, as it is hard to get an idea of their characteristics due to the large number of articles, which is rapidly increasing even for an under-resourced language such as Indonesian.

2.3 Processing pipeline

The following sketch describes how the results below were obtained:

1. URL harvesting: queries or archive/dump traversal, filtering of obvious spam and non-text documents.

2. Operations on the URL queue: redirection checks, sampling by domain name.

3. Download of the web documents and analysis: collection of host- and markup-based data, HTML code stripping, document validity check, language identification.

Links pointing to media documents were excluded from this study, as its final purpose is to enable construction of a text corpus. The URL checker removes non-http protocols, images, PDFs, audio and video files, ad banners, feeds and unwanted hostnames like *twitter.com*, *google.com*, *youtube.com* or *flickr.com*. Additionally, a proper spam filtering is performed on the whole URL (using basic regular expressions) as well as at domain name level using a list of blacklisted domains comparable to those used by e-mail services to filter spam. As a page is downloaded or a query is executed, links are filtered on-the-fly using a series of heuristics described below, and finally the rest of the links are stored.

There are two other major filtering operations to be aware of. The first concerns the URLs, which are sampled prior to the download. The main goal of this operation is strongly related to my scouting approach. Since I set my tools on an exploration course, this allows for a faster execution and provides us with a more realistic image of what awaits a potential exhaustive crawler. Because of the sampling approach, the "big picture" cannot easily be distorted by a single website. This also avoids "hammering" a particular server unduly and facilitates compliance with *robots.txt* as well as other ethical rules. The second filter deals with the downloaded content: web pages are discarded if they are too short. Web documents which are more than a few megabytes long are also discarded.

Regarding the web pages, the software fetches them from a list, strips the HTML code, sends raw text to a server instance of *langid.py* (description below) and retrieves the server response, on which it performs a basic heuristic tests.

3 Metadata

The metadata described in this section can be used in classificatory or graph-based approaches. I use some of them in the results below but did not exhaust all the possible combinations in this study. There are nine of them in total, which can be divided in three categories: corpus size metrics, which are related to word count measures, web science metrics, which ought to be given a higher importance in web corpus building, and finally the language identification, which is performed using an external tool.

[5] http://www.dmoz.org/

3.1 Corpus size metrics

Web page length (in characters) was used as a discriminating factor. Web pages which were too short (less than 1,000 characters long after HTML stripping) were discarded in order to avoid documents containing just multimedia (pictures and/or videos) or microtext collections for example, as the purpose was to simulate the creation of a general-purpose text corpus.

The page length in characters after stripping was recorded, as well as the number of tokens, so that the total number of tokens of a web corpus built on this URL basis can be estimated. The page length distribution is not normal, with a majority of short web texts and a few incredibly long documents at the end of the spectrum, which is emphasized by the differences between mean and median values used in the results below and justifies the mention of both.

3.2 Web science metrics

Host sampling is a very important step because the number of web pages is drastically reduced, which makes the whole process more feasible and more well-balanced, i.e. less prone to host biases. IP-based statistics corroborate this hypothesis, as shown below.

The deduplication operation is elementary, it takes place at document level, using a hash function. The IP diversity is partly a relevant indicator, as it can be used to prove that not all domain names lead to the same server. Nonetheless, it cannot detect the duplication of the same document across many different servers with different IPs, which in turn the elementary deduplication is able to reveal.

Links that lead to pages within the same domain name and links which lead to other domains are extracted from the HTML markup. The first number can be used to find possible spam or irrelevant links, with the notable exception of websites like Amazon or Wikipedia, which are quite easy to list. The latter may be used to assess the richness (or at a given level the suspiciousness) of a website by the company it keeps. While this indicator is not perfect, it enables users to draw conclusions without fetching all the downstream URLs.

Moreover, even if I do not take advantage of this information in this study, the fetcher also records all the links it "sees" (as an origin-destination pair), which enables graph-based approaches such as visualization of the gathered network or the assessment of the "weight" of a website in the URL directory. Also, these metadata may very well be useful for finding promising start URLs.

3.3 Language identification

I consider the fact that a lot of web pages have characteristics which make it hard for "classical" NLP approaches like web page language identification based on URLs (Baykan et al., 2008) to predict the languages of the links with certainty. That is why mature NLP tools have to be used to qualify the incoming URLs and enable a language-based filtering based on actual facts.

The language identification tool I used is *langid.py* (Lui and Baldwin, 2012). It is open-source, it incorporates a pre-trained model and it covers 97 languages, which is ideal for tackling the diversity of the web. Its use as a web service makes it a fast solution enabling distant or distributed work.

As the software is still under active development, it can encounter difficulties with rare encodings. As a result, the text gets falsely classified as for example Russian or Chinese. The languages I studied are not affected by these issues. Still, language identification at document level raises a few problems regarding "parasite" languages (Scannell, 2007).

Using a language identification system has a few benefits: it enables finding "regular" texts in terms of statistical properties and excluding certain types of irregularities such as encoding problems. Web text collections are smoothed out in relation to the statistical model applied for each language target, which is a partly destructive but interesting feature.

There are cases where the confidence interval of the language identifier is highly relevant, for instance if the page is multi-lingual. Then there are two main effects: on one hand the confidence indicator gets a lower value, so that it is possible to isolate pages which are likely to be in the target language only. On the other hand, the language guessed is the one with the largest number of identifiable words: if a given web page contains 70 % Danish and 30 % English, then it will be classified as being written in Danish, with a low confidence interval: this information is part of the metadata I associate with each web page. Since nothing particular stood out in this respect I do not mention it further.

	URLs		% in target	Length		Tokens (total)	Different IPs (%)
	analyzed	retained		mean	median		
Dutch	12,839	1,577	84.6	27,153	3,600	5,325,275	73.1
French	16,763	4,215	70.2	47,634	8,518	19,865,833	50.5
Indonesian	110,333	11,386	66.9	49,731	8,634	50,339,311	18.6
Swedish	179,658	24,456	88.9	24,221	9,994	75,328,265	20.0

Table 1: URLs extracted from search engines queries

4 Results

4.1 Characteristics of the BootCaT approach

First of all, I let my toolchain run on URLs obtained using the BootCaT approach, in order to get a glimpse of its characteristics. I let the URL extractor run for several weeks on Indonesian and Swedish and only a few days for Dutch and French, since I was limited by the constraints of this approach, which becomes exponentially slower as one adds target languages.[6] The results commented below are displayed in table 1.

The domain name reduction has a substantial impact on the set of URLs, as about a quarter of the URLs at best (for French) have different domain names. This is a first hint at the lack of diversity of the URLs found using the BootCaT technique.

Unsurprisingly, the majority of links appear to be in the target language, although the language filters do not seem to perform very well. As the adequate matching of documents to the user's language is paramount for search engines, it is probably a bias of the querying methodology and its random tuples of tokens. In fact, it is not rare to find unexpected and undesirable documents such as word lists or search engine optimization traps.

The length of web documents is remarkable, it indicates that there are likely to contain long texts. Moreover, the median length seems to be quite constant across the three languages at about 8,000 tokens, whereas it is less than half that (3,600) for Dutch. All in all, it appears to be an advantage which clearly explains why this method has been considered to be successful. The potential corpus sizes are noteworthy, especially when enough URLs where gathered in the first place, which was already too impracticable in my case to be considered a sustainable option.

The number of different IPs, i.e. the diversity in terms of hosts, seems to get gradually lower as the URL list becomes larger. The fact that the same phenomenon happens for Indonesian and Swedish, with one host out of five being "new", indicates a strong tendency.

[6]The slow URL collection is explained by the cautious handling of this free and reliable source, implying a query rate limiting on my side. The scouting approach by itself is a matter of hours.

4.2 Social networks

Due to the mixed nature of the experimental setting, no conclusions can be drawn concerning the single components. The more than 700,000 URLs that were analyzed give an insight regarding the usefulness of these sources. About a tenth of it remained as responding websites with different domain names, which is the lowest ratio of this study. It may be explained by the fast-paced evolution of microblogs and also by the potential impurity of the source compared to the user-reviewed directories whose results I describe next.

As I did not target the studied languages during the URL collection process, there were merely a few hundred different domain names to be found, with the exception of French, which was a lot more prominent.

Table 2 provides an overview of the results. The mean and median lengths are clearly lower than in the search engine experiment. In the case of French, with a comparable number of remaining URLs, the corpus size estimate is about 2.5 times smaller. The host diversity is comparable, and does not seem to be an issue at this point.

All in all, social networks are probably a good candidate for web corpora, but they require a focused approach of microtext to target a particular community of speakers.

4.3 DMOZ

As expected, the number of different domain names on the Open Directory project is high, giv-

	% in target	URLs retained	Length		Tokens (total)	Different IPs (%)
			mean	median		
Dutch	0.6	465	7,560	4,162	470,841	68.8
French	5.9	4,320	11,170	5,126	7,512,962	49.7
Indonesian	0.5	336	6,682	4,818	292,967	50.9
Swedish	1.1	817	13,807	7,059	1,881,970	58.5

Table 2: URLs extracted from a blend of social networks crawls (FriendFeed, identi.ca, and Reddit) with no language target. 738,476 URLs analyzed, 73,271 URLs retained in the global process.

ing the best ratio in this study between unfiltered and remaining URLs. The lack of web pages written in Indonesian is a problem for this source, whereas the other languages seem to be far better covered. The adequacy of the web pages with respect to their language is excellent, as shown in table 3. These results underline the quality of the resource.

On the other hand, document length is the biggest issue here. The mean and median values indicate that this characteristic is quite homogeneous throughout the document collection. This may easily be explained by the fact that the URLs which are listed on DMOZ mostly lead to corporate homepages for example, which are clear and concise, the eventual "real" text content being somewhere else. What's more, the websites in question are not text reservoirs by nature. Nonetheless, the sheer quantity of listed URLs compensates for this fact. The corpus sizes for Dutch and French are quite reasonable if one bears in mind that the URLs were sampled.

The relative diversity of IPs compared to the number of domain names visited is another indicator that the Open Directory leads to a wide range of websites. The directory performs well compared to the sources mentioned above, it is also much easier to crawl. It did not cost us more than a few lines of code followed by a few minutes of runtime to gather the URLs.

4.4 Wikipedia

The characteristics of Wikipedia are quite similar, since the free encyclopedia also makes dumps available, which are easily combed through in order to gather start URLs. Wikipedia also compares favorably to search engines or social networks when it comes to the sampling operation and page availability. It is a major source of URLs, with numbers of gathered URLs in the millions for languages like French. As Wikipedia is not a URL directory by nature, it is interesting to see what are the characteristics of the pages it links to are. The results are shown in table 3.

First, the pages referenced in a particular language edition of Wikipedia often point to web pages written in a foreign language. According to my figures, this is a clear case, all the more since web pages in Indonesian are rare. Still, with a total of more than 4,000 retained web texts, it fares a lot better than DMOZ or social networks.

The web pages are longer than the ones from DMOZ, but shorter than the rest. This may also be related to the large number of concise homepages in the total. Nonetheless, the impressive number of URLs in the target language is decisive for corpus building purposes, with the second-biggest corpus size estimate obtained for French.

The IP-related indicator yields good results with respect to the number of URLs that were retrieved. Because to the high number of analyzed URLs the figures between 30 and 46% give an insight into the concentration of web hosting providers on the market.

5 Discussion

I also analyzed the results regarding the number of links that lead out of the page's domain name. For all sources, I found no consistent results across languages, with figures varying by a factor of three. Nonetheless, there seem to be a tendency towards a hierarchy in which the search engines are on top, followed by social networks, Wikipedia and DMOZ. This is one more hint at the heterogeneous nature of the data sources I examined with respect to the criteria I chose.

This hierarchy is also one more reason why

	URLs		% in target	Length		Tokens (total)	Different IPs (%)
	analyzed	retained		mean	median		
DMOZ							
Dutch	86,333	39,627	94.0	2,845	1,846	13,895,320	43.2
French	225,569	80,150	90.7	3,635	1,915	35,243,024	33.4
Indonesian	2,336	1,088	71.0	5,573	3,922	540,371	81.5
Swedish	27,293	11,316	91.1	3,008	1,838	3,877,588	44.8
Wikipedia							
Dutch	489,506	91,007	31.3	4,055	2,305	15,398,721	43.1
French	1,472,202	201,471	39.4	5,939	2,710	64,329,516	29.5
Indonesian	204,784	45,934	9.5	6,055	4,070	3,335,740	46.3
Swedish	320,887	62,773	29.7	4,058	2,257	8,388,239	32.7

Table 3: URLs extracted from DMOZ and Wikipedia

search engines queries are believed to be fast and reliable in terms of quantity. This method was fast, as the web pages are long and full of links, which enables to rapidly harvest a large number of web pages without having to worry about going round in circles. The researchers using the BootCaT method probably took advantage of the undocumented but efficient filtering operations which search engines perform in order to lead to reliable documents. Since this process takes place in a competitive sector where this kind of information can be sold, it may explain why the companies now try to avoid giving it away for free.

In the long run, several questions regarding URL quality remain open. As I show using a high-credibility source such as Wikipedia, the search engines results are probably closer to the maximum amount of text that is to be found on a given website than the other sources, all the more when the sampling procedure chooses a page at random without analyzing the rest of a website and thus without maximizing its potential in terms of tokens. Nonetheless, confrontation with the constantly increasing number of URLs to analyze and necessarily limited resources make a website sampling by domain name useful.

This is part of my cost-efficient approach, where the relatively low performance of Wikipedia and DMOZ is compensated by the ease of URL extraction. Besides, the size of the potential corpora mentioned here could increase dramatically if one was to remove the domain name sampling process and if one was to select the web pages with the most out-domain links for the crawl.

What's more, DMOZ and Wikipedia are likely to improve over time concerning the number of URLs they reference. As diversity and costs (temporal or financial) are real issues, a combined approach could take the best of all worlds and provide a web crawler with distinct and distant starting points, between the terse web pages referenced in DMOZ and the expected "freshness" of social networks. This could be a track to consider, as they could provide a not inconsiderable amount of promising URLs.

Finally, from the output of the toolchain to a full-fledged web corpus, other fine-grained instruments as well as further decisions processes (Schäfer et al., 2013) will be needed. The fact that web documents coming from several sources already differ by our criteria does not exclude further differences regarding text content. By way of consequence, future work could include a few more linguistically relevant text quality indicators in order to go further in bridging the gap between web data, NLP and corpus linguistics.

6 Conclusion

I evaluated several strategies for finding texts on the web. The results distinguish no clear winner, complementary approaches are called for. In light of these results, it seems possible to replace or at least to complement the existing BootCaT approach. It is understandable why search engine queries have been considered a useful data source. However, I revealed that they lack diversity at some point, which apart from their impracticality may provide sufficient impetus to look for alternatives.

I discussed how I address several issues in order to design robust processing tools which (combined to the diversity of sources and usable metadata) enable researchers to get a better glimpse of the course a crawl may take. The problem of link diversity has not been well-studied in a corpus linguistics context; I presented metrics to help quantify it and I showed a possible way to go in order to gather a corpus using several sources leading to a satisfying proportion of different domain names and hosts.

As a plea for a technicalities-aware corpus creation, I wish to bring to linguists' attention that the first step of web corpus construction in itself can change a lot of parameters. I argue that a minimum of web science knowledge among the corpus linguistics community could be very useful to fully comprehend all the issues at stake when dealing with corpora from the web.

The toolchain used to perform these experiments is open-source and can be found online.[7] The resulting URL directory, which includes the metadata used in this article, is available upon request. The light scouting approach allows for regular updates of the URL directory. It could also take advantage of the strengths of other tools in order to suit the needs of different communities.

Acknowledgments

This work has been partially supported by an internal grant of the FU Berlin as well as machine power provided by the COW (COrpora from the Web) project at the German Grammar Department. Thanks to Roland Schäfer for letting me use the URLs extracted from E-Tools and DMOZ.

References

Yuki Arase and Ming Zhou. 2013. Machine Translation Detection from Monolingual Web-Text. In *Proceedings of the 51th Annual Meeting of the ACL*, pages 1597–1607.

Adrien Barbaresi. 2013a. Challenges in web corpus construction for low-resource languages in a post-BootCaT world. In Zygmunt Vetulani and Hans Uszkoreit, editors, *Proceedings of the 6th Language & Technology Conference, Less Resourced Languages special track*, pages 69–73, Poznań.

Adrien Barbaresi. 2013b. Crawling microblogging services to gather language-classified URLs. Workflow and case study. In *Proceedings of the 51th Annual Meeting of the ACL, Student Research Workshop*, pages 9–15.

Marco Baroni and Silvia Bernardini. 2004. BootCaT: Bootstrapping corpora and terms from the web. In *Proceedings of LREC*, pages 1313–1316.

Marco Baroni, Silvia Bernardini, Adriano Ferraresi, and Eros Zanchetta. 2009. The WaCky Wide Web: A collection of very large linguistically processed web-crawled corpora. *Language Resources and Evaluation*, 43(3):209–226.

E. Baykan, M. Henzinger, and I. Weber. 2008. Web Page Language Identification Based on URLs. *Proceedings of the VLDB Endowment*, 1(1):176–187.

Adam Kilgarriff, Siva Reddy, Jan Pomikálek, and PVS Avinesh. 2010. A Corpus Factory for Many Languages. In *Proceedings of LREC*, pages 904–910.

Ben King and Steven Abney. 2013. Labeling the Languages of Words in Mixed-Language Documents using Weakly Supervised Methods. In *Proceedings of NAACL-HLT*, pages 1110–1119.

Marco Lui and Timothy Baldwin. 2012. langid.py: An Off-the-shelf Language Identification Tool. In *Proceedings of the 50th Annual Meeting of the ACL*, pages 25–30.

Kevin P. Scannell. 2007. The Crúbadán Project: Corpus building for under-resourced languages. In *Building and Exploring Web Corpora: Proceedings of the 3rd Web as Corpus Workshop*, volume 4, pages 5–15.

Roland Schäfer and Felix Bildhauer. 2012. Building large corpora from the web using a new efficient tool chain. In *Proceedings of LREC*, pages 486–493.

Roland Schäfer, Adrien Barbaresi, and Felix Bildhauer. 2013. The Good, the Bad, and the Hazy: Design Decisions in Web Corpus Construction. In Stefan Evert, Egon Stemle, and Paul Rayson, editors, *Proceedings of the 8th Web as Corpus Workshop*, pages 7–15.

Jason R. Smith, Herve Saint-Amand, Magdalena Plamada, Philipp Koehn, Chris Callison-Burch, and Adam Lopez. 2013. Dirt Cheap Web-Scale Parallel Text from the Common Crawl. In *Proceedings of the 51th Annual Meeting of the ACL*, pages 1374–1383.

Vít Suchomel and Jan Pomikálek. 2012. Efficient Webcrawling for large text corpora. In Adam Kilgarriff and Serge Sharoff, editors, *Proceedings of the 7th Web as Corpus Workshop*, pages 40–44.

[7] FLUX: Filtering and Language-identification for URL Crawling Seeds – https://github.com/adbar/flux-toolchain

Focused Web Corpus Crawling

Roland Schäfer
Freie Universität Berlin
roland.schaefer
@fu-berlin.de

Adrien Barbaresi
ENS Lyon
adrien.barbaresi
@ens.lyon.org

Felix Bildhauer
Freie Universität Berlin
felix.bildhauer
@fu-berlin.de

Abstract

In web corpus construction, crawling is a necessary step, and it is probably the most costly of all, because it requires expensive bandwidth usage, and excess crawling increases storage requirements. Excess crawling results from the fact that the web contains a lot of redundant content (duplicates and near-duplicates), as well as other material not suitable or desirable for inclusion in web corpora or web indexes (for example, pages with little text or virtually no text at all). An optimized crawler for web corpus construction would ideally avoid crawling such content in the first place, saving bandwidth, storage, and post-processing costs. In this paper, we show in three experiments that two simple scores are suitable to improve the ratio between corpus size and crawling effort for web corpus construction. The first score is related to overall text quality of the page containing the link, the other one is related to the likelihood that the local block enclosing a link is boilerplate.

1 Crawl Optimization and Yield Ratios

Optimizing a crawling strategy consists in maximizing its weighted coverage $WC(t)$ at any time t during a crawl (Olston and Najork, 2010, 29), i. e., the summed weight of the documents downloaded until t, where the weight of each crawled document is calculated as a measure of the usefulness of the document relative to the purpose of the crawl. To maximize WC, it is vital to guess the weight of the documents behind harvested links before download, such that documents with potentially lesser weight have a lower probability of being downloaded. So-called focused crawlers (in a broad sense) are designed to maximize WC with respect to some specific definition of document weight, for example when documents with a high search-engine relevance (measured as its PageRank or a similar score), documents about specific subjects, or documents in a specific language are desired (Chakrabarti et al., 1999; Menczer et al., 2004; Baykan et al., 2008; Safran et al., 2012). For our purpose, i. e., web corpus crawling, a document with a high weight can simply be defined as one which is not removed from the corpus by the post-processing tools due to low linguistic quality and/or a document which contributes a high amount of text to the corpus. Recently, an interesting approach to crawl optimization along such lines was suggested which relies on statistics about the corpus yield from known hosts (Suchomel and Pomikálek, 2012). Under this approach, the weight (rather of a whole web host) is taken to be the ratio of good documents from the host remaining in the corpus after a specific post-processing chain has been applied to the documents. Harvested URLs pointing to certain hosts are prioritized accordingly. We follow a similar route like Suchomel and Pomikálek, but look at document-local features instead of host statistics.

Throughout this paper, we refer to the **yield ratio** instead of WC, although they are related notions. We define the yield ratio Y_d for a set D_c of crawled unprocessed documents and a set D_r of retained documents after filtering and processing for inclusion in a corpus, with $D_r \subset D_c$, as:

$$Y_d = \frac{|D_r|}{|D_c|} \quad (1)$$

For example, a document yield ratio $Y_d = 0.21$

means that 21% of the crawled documents survived the cleaning procedure (i. e., were not classified as duplicates or spam, were long enough, written in the target language, etc.) and ended up in the corpus. In order to maximize Y_d, 79% of the documents should not have been downloaded in the first place in this example. A parallel definition is assumed for Y_b for the respective amounts of bytes. The document yield ratio is easier to interpret because the byte yield ratio depends on the amount of markup which has to be stripped, and which might vary independently of the quality of the downloaded web pages.

Obviously, the yield ratio – like the weighted coverage – depends highly on the definition of what a good document is, i. e., what the goal of the crawl is. We assume, similar to Suchomel and Pomikálek's approach, that our tools reliably filter out documents that are interesting documents for inclusion a corpus, and that calculating a yield ratio based on the output of those tools is therefore reasonable.[1]

2 Experiment 1: Seed and Crawl Quality

In this experiment, we examine the correlation between the yield ratio of crawler seed URLs and the yield ratio of short Breadth-First Search (BFS) crawls based on those URLs. We used the Heritrix (1.14) web crawler (Mohr et al., 2004) and an older version of the `texrex` web page cleaning toolkit (Schäfer and Bildhauer, 2012). The tools perform, among other things, boilerplate detection and text quality evaluation in the form of the so-called Badness score (Schäfer et al., 2013). A document receives a low Badness score if the most frequent function words of the target language have a high enough frequency in the document. The Badness score is based on previous ideas from language identification and web document filtering (Grefenstette, 1995; Baroni et al., 2009).

Originally, this experiment was carried out in the context of an evaluation of sources of different seed URLs for crawls. In a preliminary step, we began by collecting seed URLs from various sources:

1. the *DMOZ* directory
2. the *Etools* meta search engine
3. the *FriendFeed* social service aggregator
4. the *identi.ca* social bookmarking service
5. *Wikipedia* dumps

We scraped the content behind the URLs and ran a state-of-the-art language identifier (Lui and Baldwin, 2012) on it in order to obtain language-classified seed URLs (Barbaresi, 2013).[2] We then looked specifically at the following languages associated as the single dominant language with at least one top-level domain (TLD):

1. Dutch (`.nl`)
2. French (`.fr`)
3. Indonesian (`.id`)
4. Swedish (`.se`)

We randomly sampled $1,000$ seed URLs for each of the 20 permutations of seed sources and languages/TLDs, downloaded them and used `texrex` to determine the document yield ratio for the documents behind the $1,000$ seeds. The software was configured to perform boilerplate removal, removal of documents based on high Badness scores, perfect duplicate removal, and deletion of documents shorter than $1,000$ characters (after boilerplate removal). Then, we crawled the respective TLDs, starting the crawls with the $1,000$ seed URLs, respectively. In each crawl, we downloaded 2 GB of raw data, cleaned them, and calculated the document yield ratio using the same configuration of `texrex` as we used for cleaning the seed documents. Figure 1 plots the data and an appropriate linear model.

We see that there is a strong correlation (adjusted $R^2 = 0.7831$) between the yield ratio of the documents behind the seed URLs and the yield ratio of the documents found by using the seeds for BFS crawling. It follows that giving high priority to links from pages which are themselves considered high-quality documents by the post-processing tools will likely lead to more efficient crawling. Since there is no fundamental distinction between initial URL seeds and URLs harvested at a later time during the crawl, this effect is likely to extend to the whole run time of a crawl.

[1]This claim should be backed up by forms of extrinsic/task-based evaluation (Schäfer and Bildhauer, 2013, p. 104 ff). Such an evaluation (in the form of a collocation extraction task) was recently presented for our corpora in work by Stefan Evert (Biemann et al., 2013).

[2]See also Barbaresi, this volume.

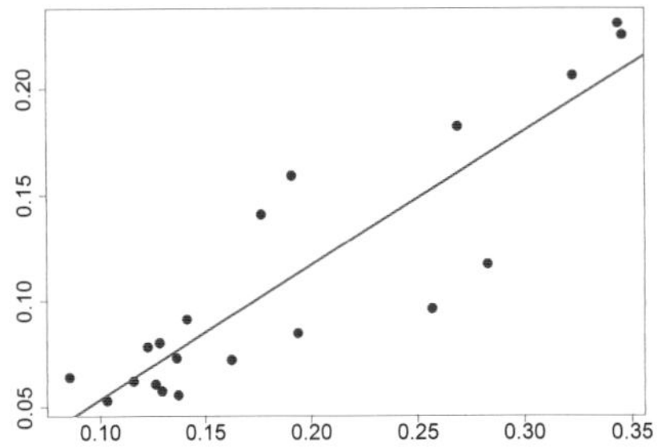

Figure 1: Yield ratio Y_d of the crawls (y axis) plotted against the yield ratio of the documents behind the crawls' 1,000 seeds (x axis). (Higher Y_d is better.) Linear model: $Intercept = -0.0098$, $Coefficient = 0.6332$, $R^2 = 0.7831$ (adjusted), $p < 0.001$ (ANOVA).

3 Experiment 2: Crawling with Cyclic URL Selection

Using the same configuration of tools as in Section 2, we performed a crawl targeting Flemish documents in the Belgian `.be` national TLD, which hosts both Flemish and French documents in substantial proportions. Usually, even under more favorable conditions (i. e., when we crawl a TLD which contains mostly documents in the target language), the yield ratio of a BFS crawl decreases rapidly in the initial phase, then staying at a low level (Schäfer and Bildhauer, 2013, p. 31). Figure 2 illustrates this with an analysis of a `.de` BFS crawl from late 2011, also processed with the same tools as mentioned in Section 2. Notice that the `.de` domain hosts German documents almost exclusively.

The interesting complication in this experiment is thus the non-target language present in the TLD scope of the crawler and the related question whether, simply speaking, predominantly Flemish documents link to other predominantly Flemish documents rather than French documents. Since the Badness score (calculated as described in Section 2) includes a form of language identification, the yield ratio takes into account this additional complication.

We tested whether the decline of the yield ratio could be compensated for by selecting "high quality" URLs in the following manner: The crawl progressed in five phases. In the first short burn-in phase, we crawled $1,000,000$ documents, and in each of the second to fifth phase, we crawled $10,000,000$ documents. After each phase, the crawl was halted, the crawler frontier was emptied, and the crawl was then re-started with a selection of the URLs harvested in the previous phase. Only those URLs were used which came from documents with a Badness score of 10 or lower (= documents in which the distribution of the most frequent function words fits the expected distribution for Flemish very well, cf. Section 2), and from text blocks with a boilerplate score (Schäfer and Bildhauer, 2012) in $[0.5, 1]$ (= likely not boilerplate). Additionally, it was made sure that no URLs were re-used between the five phases. The very promising results are plotted in Figure 3.

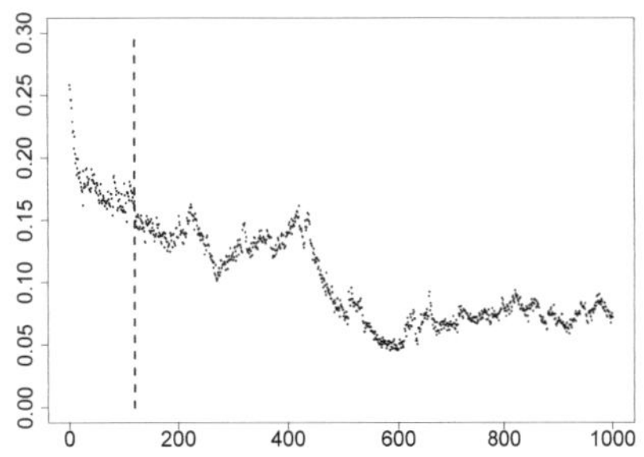

Figure 2: Yield ratio (y axis) over time for a BFS crawl in `.de` in November/December 2011 started with $231,484$ seed URLs scraped from Bing. The yield ratio was calculated at $1,000$ snapshots of 400 MB of data (= one Heritrix ARC file). For snapshots $s_1..s_{500}$: $Y_d = 0.141$, for snapshots $s_{501}..s_{1000}$: $Y_d = 0.071$. The vertical bar marks the point at which the seeds were exhausted. (Schäfer and Bildhauer, 2013, p. 31)

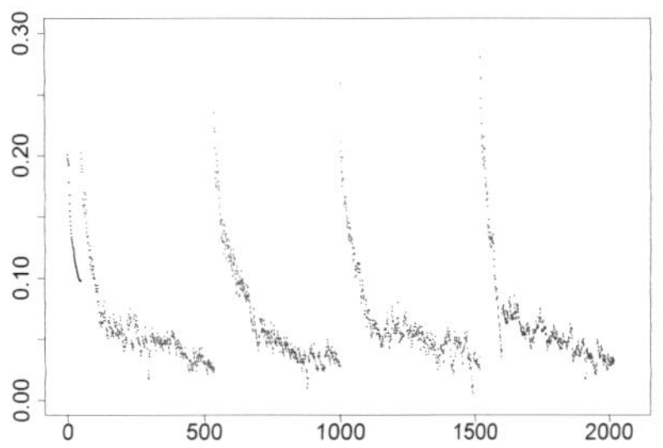

Figure 3: Yield ratio over crawl time with cyclic URL selection in the `.be` TLD. The x axis shows the crawl progression in snapshots of 400 MB of raw crawled data (= one Heritrix ARC file). The y axis shows the yield ratio for each snapshot. The five phases are clearly distinguishable by the sudden increases in yield ratio.

phase	adjusted R^2	p (ANOVA)
1	0.8288	< 0.001
2	0.9187	< 0.001
3	0.8308	< 0.001
4	0.9125	< 0.001
5	0.9025	< 0.001

Table 1: Fit of linear models for the decrease in the yield ratios of the first 100 snapshots in each of the five phases of the `.be` crawl. For the first phase, only 50 snapshots were crawled and fitted.

The decline of the yield ratio is almost linear for the first 100 snapshots in the five phases (cf. Table 1), where each phase has roughly 500 snapshots in total, and one snapshot corresponds to 400 MB of downloaded raw data. After this decline, the yield ratio remains at low levels around 0.05. Cyclic URL selection, however, repeatedly manages to push the yield ratio to above 0.2 for a short period. The subsequent sharp decline shows that link selection/prioritization should rather be implemented in the crawler frontier management in order to achieve a constant effect over longer crawls (cf. Section 5).

4 Experiment 3: Internal Crawl Analysis

For the last experiment, we used the most recent version of the `texrex` toolkit, which writes full link structures for the processed documents as a by-product.[3] An internal analysis of a small portion of a crawled data set from the German TLD was performed, which is part of the raw material of the DECOW corpus (Schäfer and Bildhauer, 2012). The data set contains 11,557,695 crawled HTML documents and 81,255,876 `http` links extracted from the crawled documents (only `<a>` tags). Among the link URLs in the sample, 711,092 are actually links to documents in the sample, so we could analyze exactly those 711,092 links. It should be noticed that we only looked at links to different hosts, such that host-internal links (navigation to "Home", etc.) are not included in the analysis.

In this experiment, we were interested specifically in the many documents which we usually discard right away simply because they are either very short (below 2 KB of unstripped HTML) or perfect duplicates of other documents. This is a step of document selection which usually precedes the cleansing used for the experiments described in Sections 2 and 3. The analysis shows that of the 711,092 link URLs in the sample, 130,703 point to documents which are not perfect duplicates of other documents and which are over 2 KB long. 580,389 of them point to documents which do not satisfy these criteria. We then evaluated the quality of the link environments in terms of their Badness and boilerplate scores. The results are shown in Figures 4 and 5.[4]

	positives	negatives
true	69,273	342,430
false	237,959	61,430

Table 2: Confusion matrix for binary download decisions based on the Badness of the document containing the URL for the DECOW crawl sample described in Section 4. Badness threshold at 10. Precision=0.225, Recall=0.530, F_1=0.316.

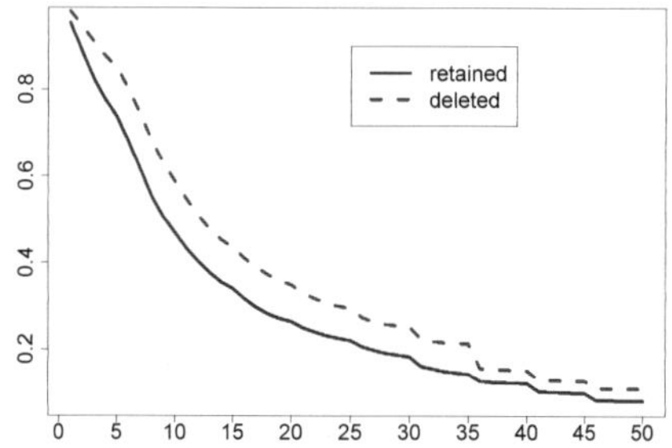

Figure 4: Badness scores of the links in the crawl analysis described in Section 4. The x axis shows the Badness scores of the documents which linked to the retained ("good") and the deleted ("bad") documents. The y axis shows the proportion of retained/deleted documents for which the Badness score is $\geq x$. (Lower Badness scores are better.)

The observable correlation between the quality of a link's context and the quality of the page behind the link is stronger for the boilerplate score than for the Badness score. For example, had we only followed links from documents with a Badness score of 10 or lower (= better), then

[3]The new version (release name `hyperhyper`) has been released and documented at `http://texrex.sf.net/`.

[4]Notice that the older version of `texrex` used in the experiments described in Sections 2 and 3 assigns a boilerplate score of 1 to text blocks which are most likely good text, while the new `texrex-hyperhyper` assigns 1 to text blocks which are most likely boilerplate. Take this into account when comparing the thresholds mentioned there and those reported here.

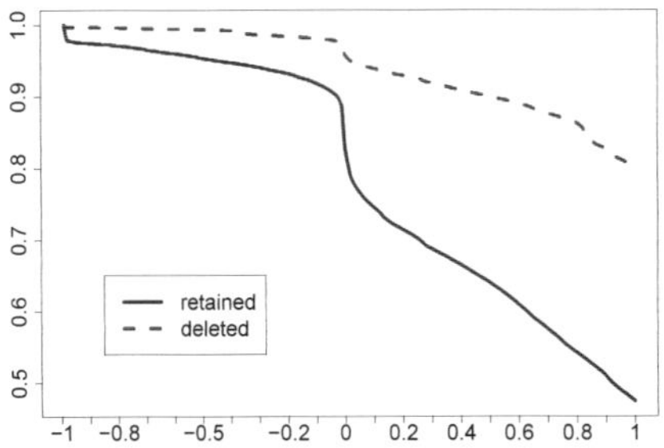

Figure 5: Boilerplate scores of the links in the crawl analysis described in Section 4. The x axis shows the boilerplate scores of the blocks which linked to the retained ("good") and the deleted ("bad") documents. The y axis shows the proportion of retained/deleted documents for which the boilerplate score is $\geq x$. (Lower boilerplate scores are better.)

	positives	negatives
true	$83,650$	$522,350$
false	$58,039$	$47,053$

Table 3: Confusion matrix for binary download decisions based on the boilerplate score of the block containing the URL for the DECOW crawl sample described in Section 4. Boilerplate threshold at 0.5. Precision=0.590, Recall=0.640, F_1=0.614.

$0.59 \times 580,389 = 342,430$ bad documents would not have been downloaded, but at the same time $0.47 \times 130,703 = 61,430$ good documents would have been lost. Tables 2 and 3 show a confusion matrix for a reasonable Badness threshold (10) and a reasonable boilerplate threshold (0.5). Obviously, if we use Badness and boilerplate scores of the link context to make a binary download decision, the accuracy is much too low, which is why we suggest to merely prioritize URLs instead of discarding them, cf. Section 5.

5 Conclusion and Planned Crawler Architecture

We have shown that two standard cleaning algorithms used in web corpus construction, i. e., text quality evaluation based on frequent short words and boilerplate detection (as implemented in the `texrex` toolkit) have a high potential for optimizing web corpus crawling through the prioritization of harvested URLs in a crawler system.

We are now in the process of designing a custom web corpus crawler system called `HeidiX`, which integrates the `texrex` post-processing tools for weight estimation based on the methods described in this paper. Cf. Figure 6, which schematically shows the current design draft.[5]

`HeidiX` is designed with a system of ranked URL back queues for harvested links (cf. *UrlQueues*). Each queue holds URLs for which the weight estimation is within a specifiable interval, such that the most promising URLs are in one queue, etc. The actual downloading is performed by massively parallel fetcher threads in the *FetcherPool*, which (in the final software) will talk to a DNS cacher and a politeness manager, which handles caching of Robots Exclusion Information and politeness intervals. The fetcher threads pop URLs from one of the ranked queues, which is selected randomly with prior probabilities inversely proportional to the rank of the queue. Thus, promising URLs are popped more often and less promising ones less often.

For guessing the weight, pluggable modules can be used and combined in the *FocusedWalker* container. Currently, we have the standard *UrlSeenFilter*, which is based on our own self-scaling Bloom Filter implementation (Bloom, 1970; Almeida et al., 2007), and which prevents any URL from being queued more than once. We have plans for a URL-based language guesser (Baykan et al., 2008) in the form of the *LanguagePredictor*, and a prioritizer based on the yield from specific hosts as described in Suchomel and Pomikálek (2012) in the form of the *HostYieldPrioritizer*, which reads statistics directly from the `texrex` module. The `texrex` module extracts all hyperlinks from processed documents and tags them with the quality scores described in this paper, such that the *QualityPrioritizer* module can adjust the expected weight of the document behind each URL.

The `HeidiX` architecture also features an alternative queueing strategy in the form of the *RandomWalker*, which allows users to obtain uniform random samples from the web based on existing algorithms (Henzinger et al., 2000; Rusmevichientong et al., 2001). Since obtaining such samples is a goal which is mostly orthogonal to the

[5]Like `texrex`, it is written entirely in the FreePascal dialect of ObjectPascal (`http://freepascal.org/`), uses only very few additional C libraries, and will be released under the GPL 3.

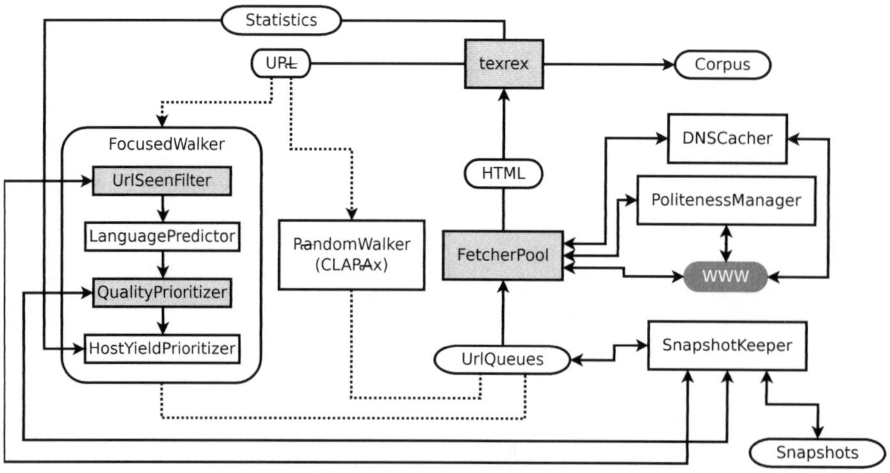

Figure 6: `HeidiX` Crawler Architecture. Grayed modules are done as of March 2014. The FocusedWalker implements an "efficiently locate good corpus document" URL prioritization scheme; the RandomWalker implements bias-corrected Random Walk URL selection for obtaining uniform random samples.

one assumed in this paper, we do not discuss this further here. Finally, a *SnapshotKeeper* module allows users to halt and continue crawls by writing/reading the current state of the relevant components to/from disk.

We hope that `HeidiX` will become a valuable tool in both the efficient construction of very large web corpora (*FocusedWalker*) and the construction of smaller unbiased reference samples as well as web analysis (*RandomWalker*).

References

Paulo Sérgio Almeida, Carlos Baquero, Nuno Preguiça, and David Hutchison. 2007. Scalable bloom filters. *Information Processing Letters*, 101:255–261.

Adrien Barbaresi. 2013. Crawling microblogging services to gather language-classified urls. workflow and case study. In *51st Annual Meeting of the Association for Computational Linguistics Proceedings of the Student Research Workshop*, pages 9–15, Sofia, Bulgaria, August. Association for Computational Linguistics.

Marco Baroni, Silvia Bernardini, Adriano Ferraresi, and Eros Zanchetta. 2009. The WaCky Wide Web: A collection of very large linguistically processed web-crawled corpora. *Language Resources and Evaluation*, 43(3):209–226.

Eda Baykan, Monika Henzinger, and Ingmar Weber. 2008. Web page language identification based on URLs. In *Proceedings of the VLDB Endowment*, pages 176–187.

Chris Biemann, Felix Bildhauer, Stefan Evert, Dirk Goldhahn, Uwe Quasthoff, Roland Schäfer, Johannes Simon, Leonard Swiezinski, and Torsten Zesch. 2013. Scalable construction of high-quality web corpora. *Journal for Language Technology and Computational Linguistics*, 28(2):23–60.

Burton Bloom. 1970. Space/time trade-offs in hash coding with allowable errors. *Communications of ACM*, 13(7):422–426.

Soumen Chakrabarti, Martin van den Berg, and Byron Dom. 1999. Focused crawling: a new approach to topic-specific web resource discovery. *Computer Networks*, 31:1623–1640.

Gregory Grefenstette. 1995. Comparing two language identification schemes. In *Proceedings of the 3rd Internation conference on Statistical Analysis of Textual Data (JADT 1995)*, pages 263–268, Rome.

Monika R. Henzinger, Allan Heydon, Michael Mitzenmacher, and Marc Najork. 2000. On near-uniform URL sampling. In *Proceedings of the 9th International World Wide Web conference on Computer Networks: The International Journal of Computer and Telecommunications Networking*, pages 295–308. North-Holland Publishing Co.

Marco Lui and Timothy Baldwin. 2012. langid.py: An Off-the-shelf Language Identification Tool. In *Proceedings of the 50th Annual Meeting of the Association for Computational Linguistics (ACL 2012)*, Jeju, Republic of Korea.

Filippo Menczer, Gautam Pant, and Padmini Srinivasan. 2004. Topical web crawlers: Evaluating adaptive algorithms. *ACM Trans. Internet Technol.*, 4(4):378–419.

Gordon Mohr, Michael Stack, Igor Ranitovic, Dan Avery, and Michele Kimpton. 2004. Introduction to Heritrix, an archival quality web crawler. In *Proceedings of the 4th International Web Archiving Workshop (IWAW'04)*.

Christopher Olston and Marc Najork. 2010. *Web Crawling*, volume 4(3) of *Foundations and Trends in Information Retrieval*. now Publishers, Hanover, MA.

Paat Rusmevichientong, David M. Pennock, Steve Lawrence, and C. Lee Giles. 2001. Methods for sampling pages uniformly from the World Wide Web. In *In AAAI Fall Symposium on Using Uncertainty Within Computation*, pages 121–128.

M.S. Safran, A. Althagafi, and Dunren Che. 2012. Improving relevance prediction for focused Web crawlers. In *IEEE/ACIS 11th International Conference on Computer and Information Science (ICIS), 2012*, pages 161–166.

Roland Schäfer and Felix Bildhauer. 2012. Building large corpora from the web using a new efficient tool chain. In Nicoletta Calzolari, Khalid Choukri, Thierry Declerck, Mehmet Uğur Doğan, Bente Maegaard, Joseph Mariani, Jan Odijk, and Stelios Piperidis, editors, *Proceedings of the Eight International Conference on Language Resources and Evaluation (LREC'12)*, pages 486–493, Istanbul. ELRA.

Roland Schäfer and Felix Bildhauer. 2013. *Web Corpus Construction*. Synthesis Lectures on Human Language Technologies. Morgan and Claypool, San Francisco.

Roland Schäfer, Adrien Barbaresi, and Felix Bildhauer. 2013. The good, the bad, and the hazy: Design decisions in web corpus construction. In Stefan Evert, Egon Stemle, and Paul Rayson, editors, *Proceedings of the 8th Web as Corpus Workshop (WAC-8)*, pages 7–15, Lancaster. SIGWAC.

Vít Suchomel and Jan Pomikálek. 2012. Effcient Web crawling for large text corpora. In Adam Kilgarriff and Serge Sharoff, editors, *Proceedings of the seventh Web as Corpus Workshop*, pages 40–44.

Less destructive cleaning of web documents by using standoff annotation

Maik Stührenberg
Institut für Deutsche Sprache / Mannheim, Germany
maik@xstandoff.net

Abstract

Standoff annotation, that is, the separation of primary data and markup, can be an interesting option to annotate web pages since it does not demand the removal of annotations already present in web pages. We will present a standoff serialization that allows for annotating wellformed web pages with multiple annotation layers in a single instance, easing processing and analyzing of the data.

1 Introduction

Using web pages as primary data for linguistic corpora often includes the procedure of cleaning and normalizing the files. Tools such as POS taggers and linguistic parsers often require the input data to be raw text, that is, without any markup at all. In addition, adding markup layers on top of an already annotated file (such as an XHTML page) often results in markup overlaps – violating XML's wellformedness constraints (Bray et al., 2008).[1]

Since the original version of the web page is the origin of every further processing, we save this version unaltered. We call this version the "raw data". As a next step we create a primary data file containing all textual information but no annotation as input for the before-mentioned linguistic processing tools.[2] Every output of a processing step is stored in a separate folder, making each step of the pipeline reproducible. However, if we want to compare multiple annotation layers, it is preferable to not have to deal with a couple of files stored in a large number of folders. To combine both the original HTML annotation and additional annotation layers, standoff annotation can be an interesting option.

[1]The discussion of this issue goes back to the days of SGML, including a large number of proposals for supporting overlapping markup not cited here due to space restrictions.

[2]Of course, this is only necessary, if the tool in question does not support pre-annotated input files.

2 Standoff annotation

Standoff annotation is the separation of primary data and markup. The concept as such is not new at all, and there are several reasons to use this approach such as read-only primary data (which is the case as well when dealing with nontextual data) or copyright restrictions. Stührenberg and Jettka (2009) discuss some existing serialization formats, including XStandoff (XSF), which we will use in this paper to demonstrate its ability to process pre-annotated documents. An XStandoff instance roughly consists of the `corpusData` root element, underneath zero or more `primaryData` elements, a `segmentation`, and an `annotation` element can occur, amongst others – see Figure 1 for a graphical overview.

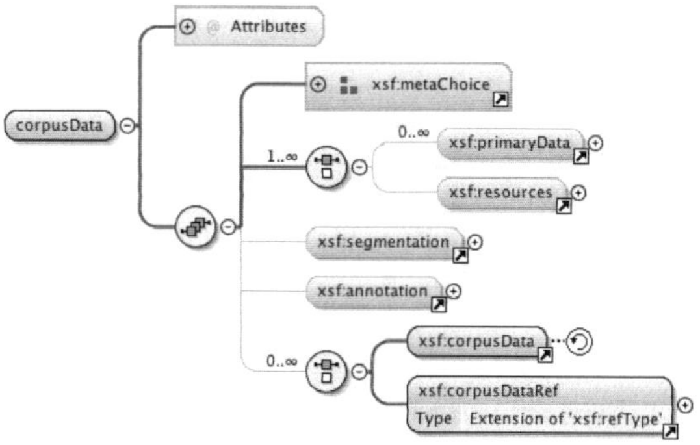

Figure 1: A graphical overview of XStandoff's root element

The two latter elements define two base constructs of standoff annotation formats: (1) the identification of regions of primary data (called segments in XStandoff) used as anchors for one or more annotations, and (2) the way in which annotations are stored.

2.1 Segmentation

In case of *textual primary data* such as web pages, segments can be identified by delimiting the character stream by means of tokenization methods (for example by splitting text into a stream of characters).

```
 T  h  i  s     i  s     a     w  o  r  d
00|01|02|03|04|05|06|07|08|09|10|11|12|13|14
```

The serialization in XStandoff can be seen below. In this example, we have selected the character span ranging from "0" to "4", resulting in the selection of the word "This".[3]

```
&lt;segment xml:id="seg_text1" primaryData="txt" type="
    char" start="0" end="4"/>
```

Since web pages consists of (Unicode) characters as well, it is possible to treat the markup as part of the character stream and in fact, this was the only way to segment primary data in XStandoff version 1 (and its predecessor SGF). However, this mechanism can be error-prone when using pre-annotated primary data because of the white space handling in XML. In this case, it is more promising to use the element node tree of an existing annotation as an initial traversal for the selection of the respective textual part. As an example we use a (valid) XHTML file, from which the first `div` element is selected by using an XPath 2.0 (Berglund et al., 2010) expression (the example can be seen in Listing 1 in Section 2.2). [4]

```
&lt;segment xml:id="seg_html1" primaryData="pd1" target
    ="xhtml:html/xhtml:body/xhtml:div[1]"/>
```

This approach is limited to work on XML instances only, that is, documents that are at least well-formed according to the XML specification, including XHTML files and those HTML5 pages that use the XHTML syntax, see Chapter 9 of the HTML5 spec (Berjon et al., 2014). Since the larger part of the World Wide Web does not fulfill this requirement, tools such as TagSoup[5] or HTML Tidy[6] can be used to pre-process those web pages. This cleaning process is less aggressive since in most cases it only results in changes of the structural markup and since we have already saved the file in its original form, destructive changes can be detected afterwards.

2.2 Annotations

Standoff annotations may be stored in the same or a different file. XStandoff, as an integrated serialization format, not only combines segmentation and all annotation layers in a single instance, but sticks as close as possible to the original inline annotation format. Element and attribute names remain unchanged as well as the tree-like structure of the element nodes. Textual element content is deleted since it can be referenced via the corresponding segment, and additional attributes are added. The converted annotation layer is stored underneath one of XStandoff's `layer` elements.[7] The document grammar (defined by an XSD 1.1 schema file) does not require the subtree underneath the `layer` element to be valid (by using the value *lax* for the `processContents` attribute of the `xs:any` element wildcard), but is has to meet the well-formedness constraints defined in the XML specification.

Using the simple XHTML page shown in Listing 1 as primary data, we can select parts of the sentence with XPath 2.0 expressions – for example, the noun phrase (and the pronoun) "This" is selected by the expression `xhtml:html/xhtml:body/substring(xhtml:div[1],1,4)` using the `substring()` function (Malhotra et al., 2010).

Listing 1: Example XHTML page

```
<html xmlns="http://www.w3.org/1999/xhtml">
 <head><title>Instance</title></head>
 <body><div>This is a word.</div></body>
</html>
```

Listing 2 shows the XStandoff instance using this XHTML page as primary data. As an annotation layer, we have added a partial POS annotation (including sentence boundary detection).

Listing 2: XStandoff instance with XHTML primary data and POS annotation

```
<corpusData xml:id="c1" xmlns="http://www.xstandoff.
    net/2009/xstandoff/1.1"
  xmlns:xsf="http://www.xstandoff.net/2009/xstandoff
    /1.1">
  <primaryData xml:id="p1">
   <primaryDataRef uri="instance.html" mimeType="
      application/xhtml+xml" encoding="utf-8"/>
```

[3]The optional `primaryData` attribute's value refers to the corresponding primary data file via XML `ID/IDREF` identity constraints ((in case of multiple primary data files – in the example to the id "txt", not via a URI. It does not provide any hint about its MIME type, this information is stored in the respective `primaryData` element shown in Listing 2.

[4]Apart from XPath, the XPointer specification defined in DeRose et al. (2002a; 2002b) and used in XCES (see (Ide et al., 2000) and Section 5) would be another option. However, since XPointer support is very sparse, XPath is a more natural fit.

[5]See `http://ccil.org/~cowan/XML/XML/tagsoup/` for further details.

[6]See `http://tidy.sourceforge.net/` for further details.

[7]XML Namespaces (Bray et al., 2009) are used to differentiate between XStandoff's markup and foreign markup.

```
  </primaryData>
  <segmentation>
    &lt;segment xml:id="seg1" target="xhtml:html/
        xhtml:body/xhtml:div[1]"/>
    &lt;segment xml:id="seg2" target="xhtml:html/
        xhtml:body/substring(xhtml:div[1],1,4)"/>
    <!-- [...] -->
  </segmentation>
  <annotation>
    <level xml:id="pos">
      <layer>
        <s xmlns="http://www.xstandoff.net/pos"
            xsf:segment="seg1">
          <np xsf:segment="seg2">
            <pron xsf:segment="seg2"/>
          </np>
          <!-- [...] -->
        </s>
      </layer>
    </level>
  </annotation>
</corpusData>
```

Additional annotation levels and layers (see Witt (2004) for a discussion about the distinction of levels and layers) can be added any time. Since XStandoff supports not only multiple annotation layers but multiple primary data files as well, there are two alternative XSF representations possible, if we extract the written text from the XHTML file and use it as primary data file: (1) The TXT file is used as additional primary data file (and serves as input for other linguistic annotation tools, see Listing 3); (2) the TXT file serves as the single primary data file and both the XHTML and the POS annotation are stored as annotation levels and layers. For the second option it is again necessary to pre-process the XHTML file with the already mentioned tools.

Listing 3: XStandoff instance with two primary data files and POS annotation

```
<corpusData xml:id="c1" xmlns="http://www.xstandoff.
    net/2009/xstandoff/1.1"
  xmlns:xsf="http://www.xstandoff.net/2009/xstandoff
      /1.1">
  <primaryData xml:id="p1">
    <primaryDataRef uri="instance.html" mimeType="
        application/xhtml+xml" encoding="utf-8"/>
  </primaryData>
  <primaryData xml:id="txt">
    <primaryDataRef uri="instance.txt" mimeType="text
        /plain" encoding="utf-8"/>
  </primaryData>
  <segmentation>
    &lt;segment xml:id="seg1" primaryData="p1" target="
        xhtml:html/xhtml:body/xhtml:div[1]"/>
    &lt;segment xml:id="seg2" primaryData="p1" target="
        xhtml:html/xhtml:body/substring(xhtml:div
        [1],1,4)"/>
    <!-- [...] -->
    &lt;segment xml:id="seg_txt1" primaryData="txt"
        start="0" end="4"/>
  </segmentation>
  <annotation>
    <level xml:id="pos">
      <layer>
        <s xmlns="http://www.xstandoff.net/pos"
            xsf:segment="seg1">
          <np xsf:segment="seg2">
            <pron xsf:segment="seg2 seg_txt1"/>
          </np>
          <!-- [...] -->
        </s>
      </layer>
    </level>
  </annotation>
</corpusData>
```

Figure 2 shows the three possible representations.

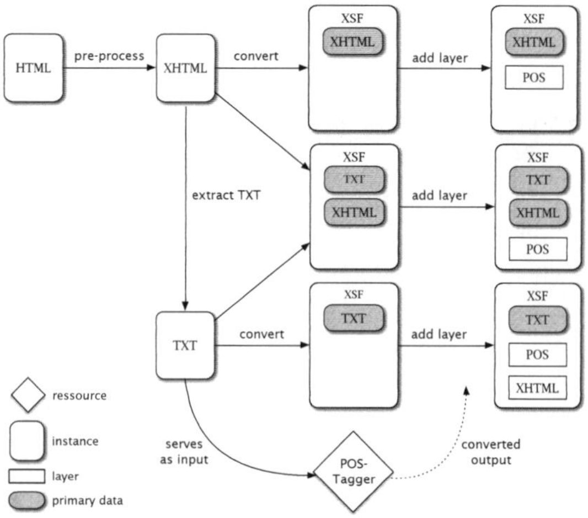

Figure 2: Possible XStandoff instances

3 Creating XStandoff instances

It it cumbersome to create XStandoff instances by hand due to its separation of primary data and annotation. In addition, most annotation tools create inline instances and can only use raw text as input files. Therefore, we have created a set of XSLT 2.0 transformation stylesheets (the XStandoff Toolkit) that allow for the easy conversion between an inline XML instance (containing a single annotation layer) to a single-layered XStandoff instance, and the merging of XStandoff instances over the very same primary data.

The XSLT stylesheet `inline2xsf` requires an input XML file ideally containing elements bound by XML namespaces since XStandoff uses XML namespaces for the layer separation (if no namespace is present, it will be generated). The process of converting an inline annotation to XSF is divided into two steps: After segments are built on the basis of the elements and the character stream of the underlying primary data, the annotation layer is produced by converting the former inline annotation and linking its elements to the according segments by `ID/IDREF` binding.

After at least two inline annotations have been transformed to single-layered XStandoff instances, it is possible to merge those into a single file. Due to the frequent use of the

ID/IDREF mechanism in XStandoff for establishing connections between segment elements and the corresponding annotation, manually merging of XStandoff files is quite unpromising. The mergeXSF XSLT stylesheet converts two XSF instances into a single one containing the annotation levels (or layers) from both input files and normalizing the corresponding segments.[8] The merge process leads to a complete reorganization of the segment list making it necessary to update the segment references of the elements in the XStandoff annotation layers. All that is done by applying the mergeXSF script.

Other stylesheets allow for the extraction and removal of single annotation layers, or a quick overview of overlapping annotations – see Stührenberg and Jettka (2009) for a detailed discussion. The current version of the stylesheet only supports the merging of two single XStandoff files at a time, additional files have to be merged successively. However, there is a web-based solution that uses the native XML database BaseX[9] as backend as well as a Java GUI that eases bulk transformation, merging and analyzing XStandoff instances.

In Jettka and Stührenberg (2011), different visualization options for concurrent markup (for example, the underlying XHTML annotation and one or more linguistic annotation layers) based on XStandoff are discussed, including newer web technologies such as WebGL for a three-dimensional visualization of overlapping subtrees. Although the examples given in this paper are quite short, Piez (2010; 2012) has already shown that the underlying concept is capable of visualizing larger instances (such as whole books) as well.

The full version of the XStandoff Toolkit can be obtained at XStandoff's website[10], although up to now it has not been adapted to support the additional segmentation mechanism for valid XHTML files described in Section 2.1.

[8]Especially this normalization can be problematic: On the one hand, there are segments spanning over the same string of the primary data (but with distinct IDs) that have to be replaced by a single segment element in the output instance. On the other hand, there are two segments with the same ID spanning over different character positions that have to get new unique IDs.

[9]See http://basex.org for further details.

[10]See http://xstandoff.net for further details.

4 Using XStandoff

The format as such has been successfully used in various projects for different purposes, such as storage format for multiple annotated corpora as part of an semi-automatic anaphora resolution (Stührenberg and Goecke, 2008), import/-export serialization of the web-based annotation tool Serengeti (Diewald et al., 2008; Poesio et al., 2011), and as annotation format for lexical chains (Waltinger et al., 2008), amongst others. Due to the fact, that the newly introduced segmentation for pre-annotated and multimodal primary data (Stührenberg, 2013) are still under development, XStandoff has not been used for larger web corpora yet.

Regarding the size of an XStandoff instance with multiple annotation layers compared to a number of inline annotation instances, it is hard to make a general expression about the increase/decrease in size. On the one hand, an XStandoff instance usually does not include the primary data (resulting in a smaller file size), on the other hand the meta information included in an XSF instance such as the additional segmentation mechanism add to the overall file size. Single heavily annotated XSF instances can take up to multiple megabytes in size, however, there have not been any problems to process these files with standard XML tools such as XSLT and XQuery. Densely annotated texts benefit from the fact that segments over a defined text span (or XHTML subtree) are only instantiated once, resulting in a state of processing in which additional annotation layer do only add very few if any segment elements to the resulting XStandoff instance. As a rule of thumb, it is highly recommended to use native XML databases such as the already-mentioned BaseX or eXist[11] as storage backends for analyzing large corpora.

5 XStandoff compared

Since the concept of standoff annotation as such is not new at all, a variety of serialization formats already exist. The most prominent candidate for a standoff serialization format supporting multiple annotations is the Graph Annotation Format (GrAF), the pivot format of the international standard ISO 24612:2012 (Linguistic Annotation Framework). However, there are different versions

[11]See http://exist-db.org for further details.

of the format: The partial document grammar in the ISO standard differs from the one that is available at its web site[12] while the first release of the GrAF-annotated Manually Annotated Sub-Corpus (MASC)[13] again uses different element and attribute names.

Another issue is that the standard is quite indifferent in terms of the segmentation over the primary data. While anchors are defined via string values, the standard states that, "[a]pplications are expected to know how to parse the string representation of an anchor into a location in the artifact being annotated" (Table 3, in the standard document). Although pre-annotated primary data is supported[14], one either may include markup as part of the character stream when referring to character positions, or use a combination of an XPath 2.0 expression to select the element containing the text, and an offset to select the corresponding part of the character string (see Section 3.3.4 of the standard) – XPath 2.0's `substring()` function shown in Listing 2 is not used.

Concerning the annotation itself, GrAF uses a feature structure format that resembles the serialization standardized in ISO 24610-1 and Chapter 18 of the TEI P5 (Burnard and Bauman, 2014). Converting existing annotation into this format can be considered as a more complex task and the resulting subtrees may become quite large (see Stegmann and Witt (2009) for a discussion of TEI feature structures as serialization for multiple annotated XML instances).

6 Conclusion and future development

Standoff annotation can be a valuable means in annotating web corpora, especially when combined with a strict policy of storing both the raw data and the primary data as non-altered files. With its segmentation mechanism supporting XPath 2.0 expressions, XStandoff can use only slightly processed XHTML pages together with their respective annotation layers, allowing for less destructive cleaning of web pages.

Since the segmentation mechanism discussed in this paper have been added to XStandoff only recently, non-textual primary data is not yet supported by the current version of the XStandoff Toolkit. Although it is much easier to identify the respective subtrees of valid XHTML pages (for example by using XPath visualization and/or selection tools such as the one included in the oXygen XML Editor[15]) compared to computing character positions, an automatic instantiation of segments is preferred. We plan to include the segmentation over pre-annotated files in one of the next iterations of the XStandoff Toolkit.

[12]See `http://www.xces.org/ns/GrAF/1.0/` for further details.

[13]See `http://www.anc.org/MASC/About.html` for further details.

[14]The preferred primary data format is raw text.

[15]See `http://oxygenxml.com` for further details

References

Anders Berglund, Scott Boag, Don Chamberlin, Mary F. Fernández, Michael Kay, Jonathan Robie, and Jérôme Siméon. 2010. XML Path Language (XPath). Version 2.0 (Second Edition). W3C Recommendation, World Wide Web Consortium.

Robin Berjon, Steve Faulkner, Travis Leithead, Erika Doyle Navara, Edward O'Connor, Silvia Pfeiffer, and Ian Hickson. 2014. Html5. a vocabulary and associated apis for html and xhtml. W3C Candidate Recommendation, World Wide Web Consortium.

Tim Bray, Jean Paoli, C. M. Sperberg-McQueen, Eve Maler, and François Yergeau. 2008. Extensible Markup Language (XML) 1.0 (Fifth Edition). W3C Recommendation, World Wide Web Consortium.

Tim Bray, Dave Hollander, Andrew Layman, Richard Tobin, and Henry S. Thompson. 2009. Namespaces in XML 1.0 (third edition). W3C Recommendation, World Wide Web Consortium.

Lou Burnard and Syd Bauman, editors. 2014. *TEI P5: Guidelines for Electronic Text Encoding and Interchange*. Text Encoding Initiative Consortium, Charlottesville, Virginia. Version 2.6.0. Last updated on 20th January 2014, revision 12802.

Steven J. DeRose, Ron Jr. Daniel, Paul Grosso, Eve Maler, Jonathan Marsh, and Norman Walsh. 2002a. XML Pointer Language (XPointer). W3C Working Draft, World Wide Web Consortium.

Steven J. DeRose, Eve Maler, and Ron Jr. Daniel. 2002b. XPointer xpointer() Scheme. W3C Working Draft, World Wide Web Consortium.

Nils Diewald, Maik Stührenberg, Anna Garbar, and Daniela Goecke. 2008. Serengeti – webbasierte Annotation semantischer Relationen. *Journal for Language Technology and Computational Linguistics*, 23(2):74–93.

Shudi (Sandy) Gao, C. M. Sperberg-McQueen, and Henry S. Thompson. 2012. W3C XML Schema Definition Language (XSD) 1.1 Part 1: Structures. W3C Recommendation, World Wide Web Consortium.

Nancy M. Ide, Patrice Bonhomme, and Laurent Romary. 2000. XCES: An XML-based Encoding Standard for Linguistic Corpora. In *Proceedings of the Second International Language Resources and Evaluation (LREC 2000)*, pages 825–830, Athens. European Language Resources Association (ELRA).

ISO/TC 37/SC 4/WG 1. 2006. Language Resource Management — Feature Structures – Part 1: Feature Structure Representation. International Standard ISO 24610-1:2006, International Organization for Standardization, Geneva.

ISO/TC 37/SC 4/WG 1. 2012. Language Resource Management — Linguistic annotation framework (LAF). International Standard ISO 24612:2012, International Organization for Standardization, Geneva.

Daniel Jettka and Maik Stührenberg. 2011. Visualization of concurrent markup: From trees to graphs, from 2d to 3d. In *Proceedings of Balisage: The Markup Conference*, volume 7 of *Balisage Series on Markup Technologies*, Montréal.

Ashok Malhotra, Jim Melton, Norman Walsh, and Michael Kay. 2010. XQuery 1.0 and XPath 2.0 Functions and Operators (Second Edition). W3C Recommendation, World Wide Web Consortium.

Wendell Piez. 2010. Towards Hermeneutic Markup: An architectural outline. In *Digital Humanities 2010 Conference Abstracts*, pages 202–205, London. The Alliance of Digital Humanities Organisations and The Association for Literary and Linguistic Computing and The Association for Computers and the Humanities and The Society for Digital Humanities – Société pour l'étude des médias interactif.

Wendell Piez. 2012. Luminescent: parsing LMNL by XSLT upconversion. In *Proceedings of Balisage: The Markup Conference*, volume 8 of *Balisage Series on Markup Technologies*, Montréal.

Massimo Poesio, Nils Diewald, Maik Stührenberg, Jon Chamberlain, Daniel Jettka, Daniela Goecke, and Udo Kruschwitz. 2011. Markup Infrastructure for the Anaphoric Bank: Supporting Web Collaboration. In Alexander Mehler, Kai-Uwe Kühnberger, Henning Lobin, Harald Lüngen, Angelika Storrer, and Andreas Witt, editors, *Modeling, Learning and Processing of Text Technological Data Structures*, volume 370 of *Studies in Computational Intelligence*, pages 175–195. Springer, Berlin and Heidelberg.

Jens Stegmann and Andreas Witt. 2009. TEI Feature Structures as a Representation Format for Multiple Annotation and Generic XML Documents. In *Proceedings of Balisage: The Markup Conference*, volume 3 of *Balisage Series on Markup Technologies*, Montréal.

Maik Stührenberg and Daniela Goecke. 2008. SGF – an integrated model for multiple annotations and its application in a linguistic domain. In *Proceedings of Balisage: The Markup Conference*, volume 1 of *Balisage Series on Markup Technologies*, Montréal.

Maik Stührenberg and Daniel Jettka. 2009. A toolkit for multi-dimensional markup: The development of SGF to XStandoff. In *Proceedings of Balisage: The Markup Conference*, volume 3 of *Balisage Series on Markup Technologies*, Montréal.

Maik Stührenberg. 2013. What, when, where? Spatial and temporal annotations with XStandoff. In *Proceedings of Balisage: The Markup Conference*, volume 10 of *Balisage Series on Markup Technologies*, Montréal.

Ulli Marc Waltinger, Alexander Mehler, and Maik Stührenberg. 2008. An integrated model of lexical chaining: application, resources and its format. In Angelika Storrer, Alexander Geyken, Alexander Siebert, and Kay-Michael Würzner, editors, *KONVENS 2008 – Ergänzungsband Textressourcen und lexikalisches Wissen*, pages 59–70, Berlin.

Andreas Witt. 2004. Multiple hierarchies: New Aspects of an Old Solution. In *Proceedings of Extreme Markup Languages*, Montréal.

Some issues on the normalization of a corpus of products reviews in Portuguese

Magali S. Duran
NILC-ICMC
University of São Paulo
Brazil
magali.duran@gmail.com

Lucas V. Avanço
NILC-ICMC
University of São Paulo
Brazil
avanco89@gmail.com

Sandra M. Aluísio
NILC-ICMC
University of São Paulo
Brazil
sandra@icmc.usp.br

Thiago A. S. Pardo
NILC-ICMC
University of São Paulo
Brazil
taspardo@icmc.usp.br

Maria G. V. Nunes
NILC-ICMC
University of São Paulo
Brazil
gracan@icmc.usp.br

Abstract

This paper describes the analysis of different kinds of noises in a corpus of products reviews in Brazilian Portuguese. Case folding, punctuation, spelling and the use of internet slang are the major kinds of noise we face. After noting the effect of these noises on the POS tagging task, we propose some procedures to minimize them.

1. Introduction

Corpus normalization has become a common challenge for everyone interested in processing a web corpus. Some normalization tasks are language and genre independent, like boilerplate removal and deduplication of texts. Others, like orthographic errors correction and internet slang handling, are not.

Two approaches to web corpus normalization have been discussed in Web as a Corpus (WAC) literature. One of them is to tackle the task as a translation problem, being the web texts the source language and the normalized texts the target language (Aw et al., 2006; Contractor et al., 2010; Schlippe et al., 2013). Such approach requires a parallel corpus of original and normalized texts of reasonable size for training a system with acceptable accuracy. The other approach is to tackle the problem as a number of sub problems to be solved in sequence (Ringlstetter et al., 2006; Bildhauer & Schäfer, 2013; Schäfer et al., 2013).

The discussion we engage herein adopts the second approach and is motivated by the demand of preprocessing a Brazilian Portuguese web corpus constituted of products reviews for the specific purpose of building an opinion mining classifier and summarizer. Our project also includes the task of adding a layer of semantic role labeling to the corpus. The roles will be assigned to nodes of the syntactic trees and, therefore, SRL subsumes the existence of layers of morphosyntactic and syntactic annotations. The annotated corpus will be used as training corpus for a SRL classifier. The aim of SRL classifier, on its turn, is to provide deep semantic information that may be used as features by the opinion miner. If the text is not normalized, the POS tagger does not perform well and compromise the parsing result, which, as consequence, may generate defective trees, compromising the assignment of role labels to their nodes.

In fact, mining opinions from a web corpus is a non-trivial NLP task which often requires some language processing, such as POS tagging and parsing. Most of taggers and parsers are made to handle error-free texts; therefore they may jeopardize the application results when they face major noises. What constitutes a major noise and which noise may be removed or corrected in such a corpus is the challenge we are facing in this project.

2. Related Work

Depending on the point of view, there are several studies that face problems similar to those faced by us. The general issue is: how to convert a non-standard text into a standard one? By non-standard text we mean a text produced by people that have low literacy level or by foreign language learners or by speech-to-text converters, machine translators or even by digitization process. Also included in this class are the texts produced in special and informal environments such as the web. Each one of these non-standard texts has its own characteristics. They may differ in what concerns spelling, non-canonical use of case, hyphen, apostrophe, punctuation, etc. Such characteristics are seen as "noise" by NLP tools trained in well written texts that represent what is commonly known as standard language. Furthermore, with the widespread use of web as corpus, other types of noise need to be eliminated, as for example duplication of texts and boilerplates.

The procedures that aim to adapt texts to render them more similar to standard texts are called normalization. Some normalization procedures like deduplication and boilerplate removal are less likely to cause destruction of relevant material. The problem arises when the noise category contains some forms that are ambiguous to other forms of the standard language. For example, the words "Oi" and "Claro" are the names of two Brazilian mobile network operators, but they are also common words ("oi" = hi; "claro" = clear). Cases like these led Lita et al. (2003) to consider case normalization as a problem of word sense disambiguation. Proper nouns which are derived from common nouns (hence, distinguished only by case) are one of the challenges for case normalization reported by Manning et al. (2008). Similar problem is reported by Bildhauer and Schäfer (2013) regarding dehyphenation, that is, the removal of hyphens used in typeset texts and commonly found in digitized texts. In German, there are many hyphenated words and the challenge is to remove noisy hyphens without affecting the correct ones. There are situations, however, in which both the corrected and the original text are desired. For example, social media corpora are plain of noises that express emotions, a rich material for sentiment analysis. For these cases, the non-destructive strategy proposed by Bildhauer and Schäfer (2013), keeping the corrected form as an additional annotation layer, may be the best solution.

3. Corpus of Products Reviews

To build the corpus of products reviews, we have crawled a products reviews database of one of the most traditional online services in Brazil, called Buscapé, where customers post their comments about several products. The comments are written in a free format within a template with three sections: Pros, Cons, and Opinion. We gathered 85,910 reviews, totaling 4,088,718 tokens and 90,513 types. After removing stop words, numbers and punctuation, the frequency list totaled 63,917 types.

Customers have different levels of literacy and some reviews are very well written whereas others present several types of errors. In addition, some reviewers adopt a standard language style, whereas others incorporate features that are typical of the internet informality, like abusive use of abbreviations, missing or inadequate punctuation; a high percentage of named entities (many of which are misspelled); a high percentage of foreign words; the use of internet slang; non-conventional use of uppercase; spelling errors and missing of diacritic signals.

A previous work (Hartmann et al. 2014) investigated the nature and the distribution of the 34,774 words of the corpus Buscapé not recognized by Unitex, a Brazilian Portuguese lexicon (Muniz et. al. 2005). The words for which only the diacritic signals were missing (3,652 or 10.2%) have been automatically corrected. Then, all the remaining words with more than 2 occurrences (5775) were classified in a double-blind annotation task, which obtained 0,752 of inter-annotator agreement (Kappa statistics, Carletta, 1996). The results obtained are shown in Table 1.

Table 1. Non-Recognized Words with more than 2 occurrences in the corpus

Common Portuguese misspelled words	44%
Acronyms	5%
Proper Nouns	24%
Abbreviations	2%
Internet Slang	4%
Foreign words used in Portuguese	8%
Units of Measurement	0%
Other problems	13%
Total	100%

The study reported herein aims to investigate how some of these problems occur in the corpus and to what extent they may affect POS tagging. Future improvements remain to be done in the specific tools that individually tackle these problems.

4. Methodology

As the same corpus is to be used for different subtasks – semantic role labeling, opinion detection, classification and summarization – the challenge is to normalize the corpus but also keep some original occurrences that may be relevant for such tasks. Maintaining two or more versions of the corpus is also being considered.

To enable a semi-automatic qualitative and quantitative investigation, a random 10-reviews sample (1226 tokens) of the original corpus was selected and POS tagged by the MXPOST tagger which was trained on MAC-Morpho, a 1.2 million tokens corpus of Brazilian Portuguese newspaper articles (Aluísio et al., 2003).

It is worthwhile to say that the sampling did not follow statistical principles. In fact, we randomly selected 10 texts (1226 tokens from a corpus of 4,088,718 tokens), which we considered a reasonable portion of text to undertake the manual tasks required by the first diagnosis experiments. Our aim was to explore tendencies and not to have a precise statistical description of the percentage of types of errors in the corpus. Therefore, the probabilities of each type of error may not reflect those of the entire corpus.

We manually corrected the POS tagged version to evaluate how many tags were correctly assigned. The precision of MXPOST in our sample is 88.74%, while its better precision, of 96.98%, has been obtained in its training corpus. As one may see, there was a decrease of 8.49% in performance, which is expected in such change of text genre.

In the sequence, we created four manually corrected versions of the sample, regarding each of the following normalization categories: spelling (including foreign words and named entities); case use; punctuation; and use of internet slang. This step produced four golden corpus samples which were used for separate evaluations. The calculation of the difference between the original corpus sample and each of the golden ones led us to the following conclusions.

The manual corrections of the sample were made by a linguist who followed some rules established in accordance with the project goals and the MXPOST annotation guidelines[1]. As a result, only the punctuation correction allowed some subjective decisions; the other kinds of correction were very objective.

5. Results of diagnosing experiments

Regarding to spelling, 2 foreign words, 3 named entities and 19 common words were detected as misspelled. A total of 24 (1.96%) words have been corrected. There are 35 words (2.90%) for which the case have been changed (6 upper to lower and 29 in the reverse direction).

Punctuation has showed to be a relevant issue: 48 interventions (deletions, insertions or substitutions) have been made to turn the texts correct, representing 3.92% of the sample. Regarding internet slang, only 3 occurrences (0.24%) were detected in the sample, what contradicted our expectation that such lexicon would have a huge impact in our corpus. However due to the size of our sample, this may have occurred by chance.

The precision of the POS tagged sample has been compared with the ones of the POS tagged versions of golden samples. The results showed us the impact of the above four normalization categories on the tagger performance.

We have verified that there was improvement after the correction of each category, reducing the POS tagger errors as shown in Table 2. When we combine all the categories of correction before tagging the sample, the cumulative result is an error reduction of 19.56%.

Table 2. Improvement of the tagger precision in the sample

Case Correction	+ 15.94%
Punctuation Correction	+ 4.34%
Spelling	+ 2.90%
Internet Slang Convertion	+ 1.45%
Cumulative Error Reduction	19.56%

These first experiments revealed that case correction has major relevance in the process of normalizing our corpus of products reviews. It is important to note that case information is largely

[1] Available at http://www.nilc.icmc.usp.br/lacioweb/manuais.htm

used as feature by Named Entities Recognizers (NER), POS taggers and parsers.

To evaluate whether the case use distribution is different from that of a corpus of well written texts, we compared the statistics of case use in our corpus with those of a newspaper corpus (http://www.linguateca.pt/CETENFolha/), as shown in Table 3.

Table 3. Percentage of case use in newspaper and products reviews corpus genres

CORPUS	Newspaper	Products Reviews
Uppercase words	6.41%	5.30%
Initial uppercase words	20.86%	7.30%
Lowercase words	70.79%	85.37%

The differences observed led us to conclude that the tendency observed in our sample (proper names and acronyms written in lower case) is probably a problem for the whole corpus.

To confirm such conclusion, we searched in the corpus the 1,339 proper nouns identified in our previous annotation task. They occurred 40,009 times with the case distribution shown in Table 4.

Table 4. Case distribution of Proper Nouns

Initial uppercase words	15,148	38%
Uppercase words	7,392	18%
Lower case words	17,469	44%
Total	40,009	100%

The main result of these experiments is the evidence that the four kind of errors investigated do affect POS tagging. In the next section we will detail the procedures envisaged to provide normalization for each one of the four categories of errors.

6. Towards automatic normalization procedures

After diagnosing the needs of text normalization of our corpus, we started to test automatic procedures to meet them. The processing of a new genre always poses a question: should we normalize the new genre to make it similar to the input expected by available automatic tools or should we adapt the existing tools to process the new genre? This is not a question of choice, indeed. We argue that both movements are needed. Furthermore, the processing of a new genre is an opportunity not only to make genre-adaptation, but also to improve general purpose features of NLP tools.

6.1 Case normalization: truecasing

In NLP the problem of case normalization is usually called "truecasing" (Lita et al, 2003, Manning et al., 2008). The challenge is to decide when uppercase should be changed into lower case and when lower case should be changed into upper case. In brief, truecasing is the process of correcting case use in badly-cased or non-cased text.

The problem is particularly relevant in two scenarios; speech recognition and informal web texts.

We prioritized the case normalization for two reasons: first, badly-cased text seems to be a generalized problem in the genre of products reviews and, second, it is important to make case normalization *before* using a spell checker. This is crucial to "protect" Named Entities from spelling corrections because when non-recognized lowercase words are checked by spellers, there is the risk of wrong correction. Indeed, the more extensive is the speller lexicon, the greater is the risk of miscorrection.

The genre under inspection presents a widespread misuse of case. By one side, lower case is used in place of uppercase in the initial letter of proper names. On the other side, upper case is used to emphasize any kind of word.

Our first tentative to tackle the problem of capitalization was to submit the samples to a Named Entity Recognizer. We chose Rembrandt[2] (Cardoso, 2012), a Portuguese NER that enhances both lexical knowledge extracted from Wikipedia and statistical knowledge.

The procedure was: 1) to submit the sample to Rembrandt; 2) to capitalize the recognized entities written in lower case; 3) to change all the words capitalized, except the named entities, to lower case. Then we tagged the sample with MXPOST to evaluate the effect on POS tagging accuracy.

The number of errors of POS tagging increased (149) when compared to the one of the sample without preprocessing (138). The

[2] The Portuguese named entity recognition is made by system Rembrandt (http://xldb.di.fc.ul.pt/Rembrandt/)

explanation for this is that among the words not recognized as named entities there were capitalized named entities which were lost by this strategy.

Next we tried a new version of this same experiment: we only changed into lower case the words not recognized as named entities that were simultaneously recognized by Unitex. The results were slightly better (143 errors) compared to the first version of the experiment, but still worse than those of the sample without preprocessing.

Our expectation was to automatically capitalize the recognized entities written in lower case. In both experiments, however, no word was changed from lower to upper case because all the entities recognized by the NER were already capitalized.

The sample contains 57 tokens of named entities (corresponding to proper nouns and acronyms) from which 24 were written in lower case. The NER recognized 22 of the 57 or 18 of the 38 types of named entities (a performance of 47.4%). Unfortunately the NER is strongly based on the presence of capitalized initial letters and was of no aid in the procedure we tested.

We argue that a finite list of known proper nouns and acronyms, although useful for improving evaluation figures, is of limited use for an application such as an opinion miner. In real scenarios this constitutes an open class and new entities shall be recognized as well.

We observed that many of the named entities found in the reviews relate to the product being reviewed and to the company that produces it. Then we realized an advantage of the source from which we have crawled the reviews: the customers are only allowed to review products that have been previously registered in the site database. The register of the name of the product is kept in our corpus as metadata for each review. This situation gave us the opportunity to experiment another strategy: to identify named entities of each review in its respective metadata file. We first gathered all the words annotated as Proper Nouns and Acronyms in our previous annotation task[3]. Then we search for the matches. The result is promising: from 1,334 proper nouns and from 271 acronyms, respectively 676 (50.67%) and 44 (16.23%) were found in the metadata. Adding both types of named entities, we have a match of 44.85% (720 of 1605). This is pretty good mainly because the named entities recognized are precisely the names of products for which opinions will be mined.

However, we still need to solve the recognition of the other named entities in order to support the truecasing strategies.

Following Lita et al. (2003) and Beaufays and Strope (2013), we are considering using a language model. Lita et al. developed a truecaser for news articles, a genre more "stable" than products reviews. Beaufays and Strope, on their turn, developed a truecaser to tackle texts generated from speech recognition. Language modeling may be a good approach to our problem because many named entities of products domain do not sound as Portuguese words. For example, they frequently have the consonants k, y and w, which are only used in proper names in Portuguese. Other approaches to truecasing reported in the literature include finite state transducers automatically built from language models and maximum entropy models (Batista et al. 2008).

6.2 Punctuation problems

Many reviews have no punctuation at all. This prevents processing the text by most of NLP tools which processes sentences. Some grammatical rules may be used to correct the use of comma, but the problem is more complex in what concerns full stop. We are now training a machine learning based program with a corpus of well written texts by using features related to n-grams. We aim at building a sentence segmentation tool which does not depend on the presence of punctuation or case folding, since these are major noises in the corpus.

6.3 Spelling correction

The common Portuguese words in the corpus which were not recognized by Unitex have been spell checked. Manual analysis is being undertaken to determine whether the word has been accurately corrected or not. Early results evidenced opportunity to extend Unitex and to improve our spellers with more phonetic rules in order to suggest more adequate alternatives. As we have already mentioned, product reviewers have several levels of literacy and those of lower level frequently swap the consonant letters that

[3] Confusion matrix of our double annotated data show that annotators diverged in what concerns Proper Nouns and Acronyms. For our purposes, however, all of them are named entities and need to be capitalized, so that this kind of disagreement did not affect the use we have made of the annotated words.

conveys the same phonetic value. For example, in Portuguese the letters "s", "c", "xc" "ss" and "ç" can have the same sound: /s/. Therefore, it is a common mistake to employ one instead of the other. These rules shall be incorporated in spell checker. In addition, there are many words which were correctly spelled, but were not part of Unitex or of the speller's dictionary or both. Both lexicons will be extended with the missing words.

In the same way, the foreign words of current use in Brazilian Portuguese shall be incorporated in the spell checkers in order to improve their suggestions of correction. As a matter of fact, foreign words are frequently misspelled. For example, "touchscreen" appeared as 10 different spelling forms in our corpus with more than 2 occurrences ("toch escreen", "touch screem", "touch sreen", "touche", "touch scream", "touchscream", "touchscreem", "touch-screen", "touchsren", "touch screen").

6.4 Internet slang normalization

Internet slang is a class that combines: 1) words written in a different way and abbreviations of recurrent expressions, for which there is an equivalent in the standard language (in this case the procedure is to substitute one for another); 2) repeated letters and punctuation (e.g. !!!!!!!!!!!, and ameiiiiiiiiiiiiiiiiiiiii, in which the word "amei" = "love" is being emphasized), which may be normalized by eliminating repetitions; and 3) sequences of letters related to emotion expression, like emoticons (e.g. ":)", ":=("), laughing (e.g. rsrsrsrs, heheheh, kkkkkkkk), which for some purposes shall be eliminated and for others shall not. The procedures relating to internet slang will be implemented carefully to allow the user to activate each one of the three procedures separately, depending on his/her interest in preserving emotion expression or not.

7. Final Remarks

This preliminary investigation about the needs of text normalization for the genre of products reviews led us to deep understand our challenges and to envisage some solutions.

We have opened some avenues for future works and established an agenda for the next steps towards corpus normalization.

Acknowledgments

This research work is being carried on as part of an academic agreement between University of São Paulo and Samsung Eletrônica da Amazônia Ltda.

References

Aluísio, S. M.; Pelizzoni, J. M.; Marchi, A. R.; Oliveira, L. H.; Manenti, R.; Marquivafável, V. (2003). An account of the challenge of tagging a reference corpus of Brazilian Portuguese. In: *Proceedings of PROPOR'2003*. Springer Verlag, 2003, pp. 110-117.

Aw, A.; Zhang, M.; Xiao, J.; Su, J. (2006). A Phrase-based Statistical Model for SMS Text Normalization. In: *Proceedings of the COLING-2006* .ACL, Sydney, 2006, pp. 33–40.

Batista, F.; Caseiro, D. A.; Mamede, N. J.; Trancoso, I. (2008). Recovering Capitalization and Punctuation Marks for Automatic Speech Recognition: Case Study for the Portuguese Broadcast News, *Speech Communication*, vol. 50, n. 10, pages 847-862, doi: 10.1016/j.specom.2008.05.008, October 2008

Beaufays, F.; Strope, B. (2013) Language Model Capitalization. In: *2013 IEEE International Conference on Acoustics, Speech and Signal Processing* (ICASSP), p. 6749 – 6752.

Bildhauer, F.; Schäfer, R. (2013) Token-level noise in large Web corpora and non-destructive normalization for linguistic applications. In: *Proceedings of Corpus Analysis with Noise in the Signal* (*CANS 2013*) .

Cardoso, N. (2012). Rembrandt - a named-entity recognition framework. In: *Proceedings of the Eight International Conference on Language Resources and Evaluation* (LREC'12). May, 23-25, Istanbul, Turkey.

Carletta, J.: Assessing Agreement on Classification Tasks: The Kappa Statistic. *Computational Linguistics*, vol. 22, n. 2, pp. 249--254. (1996)

Contractor, D.; Tanveer A.; Faruquie; L.; Subramaniam, V. (2010). Unsupervised cleansing of noisy text. *Coling 2010*: Poster Volume, pages 189–196, Beijing, August 2010.

Hartmann, N. S.; Avanço. L.; Balage, P. P.; Duran, M. S.; Nunes, M. G. V.; Pardo, T.; Aluísio, S. (2014). A Large Opinion Corpus in Portuguese - Tackling Out-Of-Vocabulary Words. In: *Proceedings of the Ninth International Conference on Language Resources and Evaluation* (LREC 2014). Forthcoming.

Lita, L., Ittycheriah, A., Roukos, S. & Kambhatla,N. (2003), Truecasing, In: *Proceedings of the 41st Annual Meeting of the Association for Computational Linguistics*, Japan.

Manning, C. D., Raghavan, P., & Schütze, H. (2008). *Introduction to information retrieval* (Vol. 1). Cambridge: Cambridge university press.

Muniz, M.C.M.; Nunes, M.G.V.; Laporte. E. (2005) "UNITEX-PB, a set of flexible language resources for Brazilian Portuguese", *Proceedings of the Workshop on Technology of Information and Human Language* (TIL), São Leopoldo (Brazil): Unisinos.

Ringlstetter, C.; Schulz, K. U. and Mihov, S. (2006). Orthographic Errors in Web Pages: Toward Cleaner Web Corpora. In: *Computational Linguistics* Volume 32, Number 3, p. 295-340.

Schäfer, R.; Barbaresi, A.; Bildhauer, F. (2013) The Good, the Bad, and the Hazy: Design Decisions in Web Corpus Construction. In: *Proceedings of the 8th Web as Corpus Workshop* (WAC-8).

Schlippe, T.; Zhu, C.; Gebhardt J.;, Schultz, T.(2013). Text Normalization based on Statistical Machine Translation and Internet User Support. In: *Proceedings of The 38th International Conference on Acoustics, Speech, and Signal Processing* (ICASSP-2013) p. 8406 – 841.

{bs,hr,sr}WaC – Web corpora of Bosnian, Croatian and Serbian

Nikola Ljubešić
University of Zagreb
Ivana Lučića 3, 10000 Zagreb, Croatia
nljubesi@ffzg.hr

Filip Klubička
University of Zagreb
Ivana Lučića 3, 10000 Zagreb, Croatia
fklubick@ffzg.hr

Abstract

In this paper we present the construction process of top-level-domain web corpora of Bosnian, Croatian and Serbian. For constructing the corpora we use the SpiderLing crawler with its associated tools adapted for simultaneous crawling and processing of text written in two scripts, Latin and Cyrillic. In addition to the modified collection process we focus on two sources of noise in the resulting corpora: 1. they contain documents written in the other, closely related languages that can not be identified with standard language identification methods and 2. as most web corpora, they partially contain low-quality data not suitable for the specific research and application objectives. We approach both problems by using language modeling on the crawled data only, omitting the need for manually validated language samples for training. On the task of discriminating between closely related languages we outperform the state-of-the-art Blacklist classifier reducing its error to a fourth.

1 Introduction

Building web corpora for various NLP tasks has become quite a standard approach, especially if funding is limited and / or there is need for large amounts of textual data.

Although off-the-shelf solutions for compiling web corpora have emerged recently, there are still specific challenges that have to be addressed in most corpus construction processes. One such challenge that we face while constructing the corpora described in this paper is simultaneous usage of two scripts on two out of three top-level domains (TLDs) crawled.

Additionally, there are still many open questions and possibilities for improvement in the process of collecting data as well as data post-processing. We address two of the latter kind – discrimination between similar, neighboring languages that are used on all selected TLDs, and the question of text quality in corpora collected in such a fully automated fashion.

In the paper we present the process of building web corpora of Bosnian, Croatian and Serbian by crawling the `.ba`, `.hr` and `.rs` TLDs. The three languages belong to the South Slavic language branch and are very similar to each other. The biggest differences between Croatian and Serbian are the proto-Slavic vowel *jat* (Croatian *čovjek* vs. Serbian *čovek*), way of handling proper nouns (Croatian *New York* vs. Serbian *Nju Jork*), specific syntactic constructions (Croatian *hoću raditi* vs. Serbian *hoću da radim*) and a series of lexical differences (Croatian *mrkva* vs. Serbian *šargarepa*). Bosnian is mostly seen as a mixture of those two and allows, beside its own lexical specificities, solutions from one or both languages.[1]

This paper is structured as follows: in Section 2 we give an overview of related work regarding existing (web) corpora of the languages in question, language identification and web text quality estimation. Section 3 shows the process of collecting the three TLD corpora with emphasis on the problem of collecting data written in various scripts, while in Section 4 we describe the linguistic annotation layers added to the corpora. Section 5 depicts our approach to discriminating between very similar languages while in Section 6 we describe our approach to identifying documents of low text quality, and both approaches use recently crawled data only.

[1] A more thorough comparison of the three languages is available at `http://en.wikipedia.org/wiki/Comparison_of_standard_Bosnian,_Croatian_and_Serbian`

2 Related work

The only two South Slavic languages for which web corpora were previously built are Croatian and Slovene (Ljubešić and Erjavec, 2011). The Croatian corpus presented in this paper is actually an extension of the existing corpus, representing its second version. hrWaC v1.0 was, until now, the biggest available corpus of Croatian.

For Bosnian, almost no corpora are available except the SETimes corpus[2], which is a 10-languages parallel corpus with its Bosnian side consisting of 2.2 million words, and The Oslo Corpus of Bosnian Texts[3], which is a 1.5 million words corpus consisting of different genres of texts that were published in the 1990s.

For the Serbian language, until now, the largest corpus was the SrpKor corpus[4], consisting of 118 million words that are annotated with part-of-speech information (16 tags) and lemmatized. The corpus is available for search through an interface for non-commercial purposes.

Until now, no large freely downloadable corpora of Bosnian and Serbian were available, and this was one of the strongest motivations for our work.

Multiple pipelines for building web corpora were described in many papers in the last decade (Baroni et al., 2009; Ljubešić and Erjavec, 2011; Schäfer and Bildhauer, 2012), but, to the best of our knowledge, only one pipeline is freely available as a complete, ready-to-use tool: the Brno pipeline (Suchomel and Pomikálek, 2012), consisting of the SpiderLing crawler[5], the Chared encoding detector[6], the jusText content extractor[7] and the Onion near-deduplicator[8]. Although we have our own pipeline set up (this is the pipeline the first versions of hrWaC and slWaC were built with), we decided to compile these versions of web corpora with the Brno pipeline for two reasons: 1. to inspect the pipeline's capabilities, and 2. to extend the Croatian web corpus as much as possible by using a different crawler.

Although language identification is seen as a solved problem by many, the recently growing interest for it indicates the opposite. Recently, researchers focused on improving off-the-shelf tools for identifying many languages (Lui and Baldwin, 2012), discriminating between similar languages where standard tools fail (Tiedemann and Ljubešić, 2012), identifying documents written in multiple languages and identifying the languages in such multilingual documents (Lui et al., 2014).

Text quality in automatically constructed web corpora is quite an underresearched topic, with the exception of boilerplate removal / content extraction approaches that deal with this problem implicitly (Baroni et al., 2008; Kohlschütter et al., 2010), but quite drastically, by removing all content that does not conform to the criteria set. A recent approach to assessing text quality in web corpora in an unsupervised manner (Schäfer et al., 2013) calculates the weighted mean and standard deviation of n most frequent words in a corpus sample and measures how much a specific document deviates from the estimated means. This approach is in its basic idea quite similar to ours because it assumes that most of the documents in the corpus contain content of good quality. The main difference in our approach is that we do not constrain ourselves to most frequent words as features, but use character and word n-grams of all available text.

3 Corpus construction

For constructing the corpora we used the SpiderLing crawler[9] along with its associated tools for encoding guessing, content extraction, language identification and near-duplicate removal (Suchomel and Pomikálek, 2012). Seed URLs for Bosnian and Serbian were obtained via the Google Search API queried with bigrams of mid-frequency terms. Those terms were obtained from corpora that were built with focused crawls of newspaper sites as part of our previous research (Tiedemann and Ljubešić, 2012). For Croatian seed URLs, we used the home pages of web domains obtained during the construction of the first version of the hrWaC corpus. The number of seed URLs was 8,388 for bsWaC, 11,427 for srWaC and 14,396 for hrWaC. Each TLD was crawled for 21 days with 16 cores used for document processing.

Because Serbian – which is frequently used on the Serbian and Bosnian TLDs – uses two scripts

[2] http://nlp.ffzg.hr/resources/corpora/setimes/

[3] http://www.tekstlab.uio.no/Bosnian/Corpus.html

[4] http://tinyurl.com/mocnzna

[5] http://nlp.fi.muni.cz/trac/spiderling

[6] https://code.google.com/p/chared/

[7] http://code.google.com/p/justext/

[8] http://code.google.com/p/onion/

[9] http://nlp.fi.muni.cz/trac/spiderling

– Latin and Cyrillic – we had to adjust the standard corpus construction process to cope with both scripts. This was done by 1. building new two-script models for encoding guessing with Chared, 2. defining stop-words used in content extraction in both scripts and 3. transforming extracted text from Cyrillic to Latin with *serbian.py*[10] before performing language identification and duplicate removal. We kept all content of the final corpora in the Latin script to simplify further processing, especially because linguistic annotation layers were added with models developed for Croatian which uses the Latin script exclusively. The information about the amount of Cyrillic text in each document is still preserved as an attribute of the `<doc>` element. Overall the percentage of documents written >90% in the Cyrillic script was 3.2% on the Bosnian TLD and 16.7% on the Serbian TLD.

Near-duplicate identification was performed both on the document and the paragraph level. The document-level near-duplicates were removed from the corpus cutting its size in half, while paragraph-level near-duplicates were labeled by the `neardupe` binary attribute in the `<p>` element enabling the corpus users to decide what level of near-duplicate removal suits their needs.

The resulting size of the three corpora (in millions of tokens) after each of the three duplicate removal stages is given in Table 1. Separate numbers are shown for the new crawl of the Croatian TLD and the final corpus consisting of both crawls.

	PHYS	DOCN	PARN
bsWaC 1.0	722	429	288
hrWaC new	1,779	1,134	700
hrWaC 2.0	2,686	1,910	1,340
srWaC 1.0	1,554	894	557

Table 1: Size of the corpora in Mtokens after physical duplicate (PHY), document near-duplicate (DOCN) and paragraph near-duplicate removal (PARN)

At this point of the corpus construction process the `<doc>` element contained the following attributes:

- `domain` – the domain the document is published on (e.g. `zkvh.org.rs`)
- `url` – the URL of the document
- `crawl_date` – date the document was crawled
- `cyrillic_num` – number of Cyrillic letters in the document
- `cyrillic_perc` – percentage of letters that are Cyrillic

4 Corpus annotation

We annotated all three corpora on the level of lemmas, morphosyntactic description (675 tags) and dependency syntax (15 tags). Lemmatization was performed with the CST's Lemmatiser[11] (Jongejan and Dalianis, 2009), morphosyntactic tagging with HunPos[12] (Halácsy et al., 2007) and dependency syntax with mate-tools[13] (Bohnet, 2010). All models were trained on the Croatian 90k-token annotated corpus SETimes.HR[14] (Agić and Ljubešić, 2014) that we recently expanded with 50k additional tokens from various newspaper domains (at this point we call it simply SETimes.HR+). Although the annotated training corpora are Croatian, previous research (Agić et al., 2013a; Agić et al., 2013b) has shown that on this level of tagging accuracy on in-domain test sets (lemma ≈96%, morphosyntactic description (MSD) ≈87%, labeled attachment score (LAS) ≈73%), annotating Serbian text with models trained on Croatian data produced performance loss of only up to 3% on all three levels of annotation, while on out-of-domain test sets (lemma ≈92%, MSD ≈81%, LAS ≈65%) there was no loss in accuracy.

We nevertheless performed an intervention in the SETimes.HR+ corpus before training the models used for annotating the Bosnian and the Serbian TLD corpora. Namely, on the morphosyntactic level the tagsets of Croatian and Serbian are identical, except for one subset of tags for the future tense which is present in Serbian and not present in Croatian. This is because Croatian uses the complex, analytic future tense consisting of the infinitive of the main verb and the present tense of the auxiliary verb *have* (*radit ćemo*) while Serbian uses both the analytic and the synthetic form where the two words are conflated into one (*radićemo*).

[10] `http://klaus.e175.net/code/serbian.py`

[11] `https://github.com/kuhumcst/cstlemma`

[12] `https://code.google.com/p/hunpos/`

[13] `https://code.google.com/p/mate-tools/`

[14] `http://nlp.ffzg.hr/resources/corpora/setimes-hr/`

To enable models to correctly handle both the analytic and synthetic form of the future tense, we simply repeated the sentences containing the analytic form that we automatically transformed to the synthetic one. By annotating the bsWaC and srWaC corpora with the models trained on the modified SETimes.HR+ corpus, we annotated 610k word forms in srWaC and 115k word forms in bsWaC with the synthetic future tense. Manual inspection showed that most of the tokens actually do represent the future tense, proving that the intervention was well worth it.

The lemmatization and morphosyntactic annotation of all three corpora took just a few hours while the full dependency parsing procedure on 40 server grade cores took 25 days.

5 Language identification

Because each of the three languages of interest is used to some extent on each of the three TLDs and, additionally, these languages are very similar, discriminating between them presented both a necessity and a challenge.

In previous work on discriminating between closely related languages, the Blacklist (BL) classifier (Tiedemann and Ljubešić, 2012) has shown to be, on a newspaper-based test set, 100% accurate in discriminating between Croatian and Serbian, and 97% accurate on all three languages of interest.

Our aim at this stage was twofold: 1. to put the existing BL classifier on a realistic test on (noisy) web data and 2. to propose an alternative, simple, data-intense, but noise-resistant method which can be used for discriminating between closely related languages or language varieties that are predominantly used on specific sections of the Web.

Our method (LM1) uses the whole content of each of the three TLD web corpora (so large amounts of automatically collected, noisy data) to build unigram-level language models. Its advantage over the BL classifier is that it does not require any clean, manually prepared samples for training. The probability estimate for each word w given the TLD, using add-one smoothing is this:

$$\hat{P}(w|TLD) = \frac{c(w, TLD) + 1}{\sum_{w_i \in V}(c(w_i, TLD) + 1)} \quad (1)$$

where $c(w, TLD)$ is the number of times word w occurred on the specific TLD and V is the vocabulary defined over all TLDs.

We perform classification on each document as a *maximum-a-posteriori* (MAP) decision, i.e. we choose the language of the corresponding TLD ($l \in TLD$) that produces maximum probability with respect to words occurring in the document ($w_1 ... w_n$):

$$l_{map} = \arg\max_{l \in TLD} \prod_{i=1..n} \hat{P}(w_i|l) \quad (2)$$

We should note here that our approach is identical to using the Naïve Bayes classifier without the *a priori* probability for each class, i.e. language.

Speaking in loose terms, what we do is that for each document of each TLD, we identify, on the word level, to which TLD data collection the document corresponds best.

Because Bosnian is mostly a mixture of Croatian and Serbian and actually represents a continuum between those two languages, we decided to compare the BL and the LM1 classifier on a much more straight-forward task of discriminating between Croatian and Serbian. The results of classifying each document with both classifiers are given in Table 2. They show that both classifiers agree on around 75% of decisions and that around 0.4 percent of documents from hrWaC are identified as Serbian and 1.5 percent of document from srWaC as Croatian.

	BL	LM1	agreement
hrWaC	0.42%	0.3%	73.15%
srWaC	1.93 %	1.28%	80.53%

Table 2: Percentage of documents identified by each classifier as belonging to the other language

We compared the classifiers by manually inspecting 100 random documents per corpus where the two classifiers were not in agreement. The results of this tool-oriented evaluation are presented in Table 3 showing that the LM1 classifier produced the correct answer in overall 4 times more cases than the BL classifier.

If we assume that the decisions where the two classifiers agree are correct (and manual inspection of data samples points in that direction) we can conclude that our simple, data-intense, noise-resistant LM1 method cuts the BL classification error to a fourth. We consider a more thorough evaluation of the two classifiers, probably by pooling and annotating documents that were identified

	BL	LM1	NA
hrWaC	18%	62%	20%
srWaC	10%	48%	42%

Table 3: Percentage of correct decisions of each classifier on documents where the classifiers disagreed (NA represents documents that are a mixture of both languages)

as belonging to the other TLD language by some classifier, as future work.

Due to the significant reduction in error by the LM1 classifier, we annotated each document in the hrWaC and srWaC corpora with the LM1 binary hr-sr language identifier while on bsWaC we used the LM1 ternary bs-hr-sr classifier. This decision is based on the fact that discriminating between all three languages is very hard even for humans and that for most users the hr-sr discrimination on the two corpora will be informative enough. In each document we encoded the normalized distribution of log-probabilities for the considered languages, enabling the corpus user to redefine his own language criterion.

The percentage of documents from each corpus being identified as a specific language is given in Table 4.

	bs	hr	sr
bsWaC	78.0%	16.5%	5.5%
hrWaC	-	99.7%	0.3%
srWaC	-	1.3%	98.7%

Table 4: Distribution of identified languages throughout the three corpora

Additional attributes added to the `<doc>` element during language identification are these:

- `lang` – language code of the language identified by maximum-a-posteriori
- `langdistr` – normalized distribution of log probabilities of languages taken under consideration (e.g. `bs:-0.324|hr:-0.329|sr:-0.347` for a document from bsWaC)

6 Identifying text of low quality

Finally, we tackled the problem of identifying documents of low text quality in an unsupervised manner by assuming that most of the content of each web corpus is of good quality and that low quality content can be identified as data points of lowest probability regarding language models built on the whole data collection. We pragmatically define low quality content as content not desirable for a significant number of research or application objectives.

For each TLD we calculated character n-gram and word n-gram language models in the same manner as in the previous section (Equation 1) for language identification. We scored each TLD document with each language model that was built on that TLD. To get a probability estimate which does not depend on the document length, we calculated probabilities of subsequences of identical length and computed the average of those.

We manually inspected documents with low probability regarding character n-gram models from level 1 to level 15 and word n-gram models from level 1 to level 5. Word n-gram models proved to be much less appropriate for capturing low quality documents by lowest probability scores than character n-gram models. Among character n-gram models, 3-gram models were able to identify documents with noise on the token level while 12-gram models assigned low probabilities to documents with noise above the token level.

The most frequent types of potential noise found in lowest scored documents in all three corpora are the following:

- 3-gram models
  - non-standard usage of uppercase, lowercase and punctuation
  - URL-s
  - uppercase want ads
  - formulas
- 12-gram models
  - words split into multiple words (due to soft hyphen usage or HTML tags inside words)
  - enumerated and bulleted lists
  - uppercase want ads
  - non-standard text (slang, no uppercased words, emoticons)
  - dialects
  - lyric, epic, historical texts

The character 3-gram method has additionally proven to be a very good estimate of text quality on the lexical level by strongly correlating (0.74) with the knowledge-heavy method of calculating lexical overlap of each document with a morphological dictionary which is available for Croatian[15].

An interesting finding is that word-level models perform much worse for this task than character-level models. We hypothesize that this is due to feature space sparsity on the word level which is much lower on the character level.

We decided to postpone any final decisions (like discretizing these two variables and defining one or two categorical ones) and therefore encoded both log-probabilities as attributes in each document element in the corpus leaving to the final users to define their own cut-off criteria. To make that decision easier, for each document and each character n-gram method we computed the percentage of documents in the corpus that have an equal or lower result of that character n-gram method. This makes removing a specific percentage of documents with lowest scores regarding a method much easier.

We also computed one very simple estimate of text quality – the percentage of characters that are diacritics. Namely, for some tasks, like lexicon enrichment, working on non-diacritized text is not an option. Additionally, it is to expect that lower usage of diacritics points to less standard language usage. The distribution of this text quality estimate in the hrWaC corpus (all three corpora follow the same pattern) is depicted in Figure 1 showing that the estimate is rather normally distributed with a small peak at value zero representing non-diacritized documents.

In each <doc> element we finally encoded 5 attributes regarding text quality:

- `3graph` – average log-probability on 100-character sequences regarding the character 3-gram model trained on the whole TLD corpus
- `3graph_cumul` – percentage of documents with equal or lower `3graph` attribute value
- `12graph` – same as `3graph`, but computed with the character 12-gram model
- `12graph_cumul` – like `3graph_cumul`, but for the `12graph` attribute

[15]`http://bit.ly/1mRjMrP`

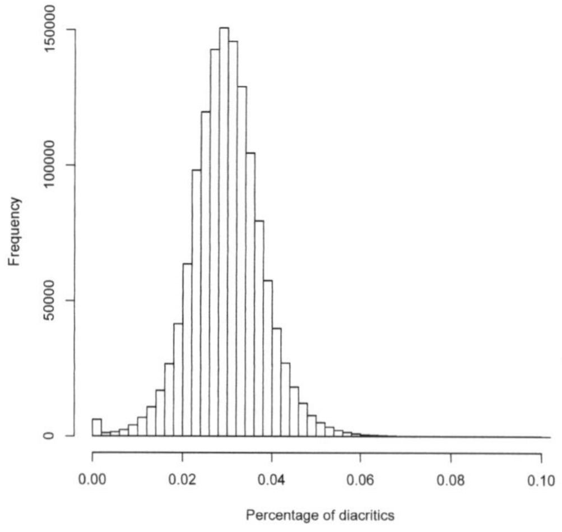

Figure 1: Distribution of the percentage of characters of a document being diacritics

- `diacr_perc` – percentage of non-whitespace characters that are diacritics

We plan to perform extrinsic evaluation of the three estimates of text quality on various NLP tasks such as language modeling for statistical machine translation, morphological lexicon induction, distributional lexicon induction of closely related languages and multi-word expression extraction.

7 Conclusion

In this paper we described the process of constructing three TLD corpora of Bosnian, Croatian and Serbian.

After presenting the construction and annotation process of the largest existing corpora for each of the three languages, we focused on the issue that all three languages are to some extent used on all three TLDs. We presented a method for discriminating between similar languages that is based on unigram language modeling on the crawled data only, which exploits the fact that the majority of the data published on each TLD is written in the language corresponding to that TLD. We reduced the error of a state-of-the-art classifier to a fourth on documents where the two classifiers disagree on.

We dealt with the problem of identifying low quality content as well, again using language modeling on crawled data only, showing that document probability regarding a character 3-gram model is a very good estimate of lexical quality, while low character 12-gram probabilities identify low quality documents beyond the word boundary.

We encoded a total of 12 attributes in the document element and the paragraph-near-duplicate information in the paragraph element enabling each user to search for and define his own criteria.

We plan on experimenting with those attributes on various tasks, from language modeling for statistical machine translation, to extracting various linguistic knowledge from those corpora.

Acknowledgement

The research leading to these results has received funding from the European Union Seventh Framework Programme FP7/2007-2013 under grant agreement no. PIAP-GA-2012-324414 (project Abu-MaTran).

References

[Agić and Ljubešić2014] Željko Agić and Nikola Ljubešić. 2014. The SETimes.HR linguistically annotated corpus of Croatian. In *Proceedings of LREC 2014.*

[Agić et al.2013a] Željko Agić, Nikola Ljubešić, and Danijela Merkler. 2013a. Lemmatization and morphosyntactic tagging of Croatian and Serbian. In *Proceedings of the 4th Biennial International Workshop on Balto-Slavic Natural Language Processing*, pages 48–57, Sofia, Bulgaria, August. Association for Computational Linguistics.

[Agić et al.2013b] Željko Agić, Danijela Merkler, and Daša Berović. 2013b. Parsing Croatian and Serbian by using Croatian dependency treebanks. In *Proceedings of the Fourth Workshop on Statistical Parsing of Morphologically Rich Languages (SPMRL 2013).*

[Baroni et al.2008] Marco Baroni, Francis Chantree, Adam Kilgarriff, and Serge Sharoff. 2008. Cleaneval: a competition for cleaning web pages. In *Proceedings of the Sixth International Language Resources and Evaluation (LREC'08)*, Marrakech, Morocco. European Language Resources Association (ELRA).

[Baroni et al.2009] Marco Baroni, Silvia Bernardini, Adriano Ferraresi, and Eros Zanchetta. 2009. The WaCky wide web: a collection of very large linguistically processed web-crawled corpora. *Language Resources and Evaluation*, pages 209–226.

[Bohnet2010] Bernd Bohnet. 2010. Very high accuracy and fast dependency parsing is not a contradiction. In *The 23rd International Conference on Computational Linguistics (COLING 2010).*

[Halácsy et al.2007] Péter Halácsy, András Kornai, and Csaba Oravecz. 2007. HunPos: an open source trigram tagger. In *Proceedings of the 45th Annual Meeting of the ACL on Interactive Poster and Demonstration Sessions*, ACL '07, pages 209–212, Stroudsburg, PA, USA. Association for Computational Linguistics.

[Jongejan and Dalianis2009] Bart Jongejan and Hercules Dalianis. 2009. Automatic training of lemmatization rules that handle morphological changes in pre-, in- and suffixes alike. In *Proceedings of the Joint Conference of the 47th Annual Meeting of the ACL and the 4th International Joint Conference on Natural Language Processing of the AFNLP*, pages 145–153.

[Kohlschütter et al.2010] Christian Kohlschütter, Peter Fankhauser, and Wolfgang Nejdl. 2010. Boilerplate detection using shallow text features. In Brian D. Davison, Torsten Suel, Nick Craswell, and Bing Liu, editors, *WSDM*, pages 441–450. ACM.

[Ljubešić and Erjavec2011] Nikola Ljubešić and Tomaž Erjavec. 2011. hrWaC and slWac: Compiling Web Corpora for Croatian and Slovene. In *Text, Speech and Dialogue - 14th International Conference, TSD 2011, Pilsen, Czech Republic*, Lecture Notes in Computer Science, pages 395–402. Springer.

[Lui and Baldwin2012] Marco Lui and Timothy Baldwin. 2012. langid.py: An off-the-shelf language identification tool. In *ACL (System Demonstrations)*, pages 25–30.

[Lui et al.2014] Marco Lui, Jey Han Lau, and Timothy Baldwin. 2014. Automatic detection and language identification of multilingual documents. *Transactions of the Association for Computational Linguistics.*

[Schäfer and Bildhauer2012] Roland Schäfer and Felix Bildhauer. 2012. Building large corpora from the web using a new efficient tool chain. In *Proceedings of the Eight International Conference on Language Resources and Evaluation (LREC'12)*, Istanbul, Turkey. European Language Resources Association (ELRA).

[Schäfer et al.2013] Roland Schäfer, Adrien Barbaresi, and Felix Bildhauer. 2013. The good, the bad, and the hazy: Design decisions in web corpus construction. In *Proceedings of the 8th Web as Corpus Workshop (WAC8).*

[Suchomel and Pomikálek2012] Vít Suchomel and Jan Pomikálek. 2012. Efficient web crawling for large text corpora. In Serge Sharoff Adam Kilgarriff, editor, *Proceedings of the seventh Web as Corpus Workshop (WAC7)*, pages 39–43, Lyon.

[Tiedemann and Ljubešić2012] Jörg Tiedemann and Nikola Ljubešić. 2012. Efficient discrimination between closely related languages. In *Proceedings of COLING 2012*, pages 2619–2634, Mumbai, India.

The *PAISÀ* Corpus of Italian Web Texts

Verena Lyding * verena.lyding@eurac.edu

Egon Stemle* egon.stemle@eurac.edu

Claudia Borghetti† claudia.borghetti@unibo.it

Marco Brunello‡ marcobrunello84@gmail.com

Sara Castagnoli† s.castagnoli@unibo.it

Felice Dell'Orletta§ felice.dellorletta@ilc.cnr.it

Henrik Dittmann¶ henrik.dittmann@bordet.be

Alessandro Lenci|| alessandro.lenci@ling.unipi.it

Vito Pirrelli§ vito.pirrelli@ilc.cnr.it

Abstract

PAISÀ is a Creative Commons licensed, large web corpus of contemporary Italian. We describe the design, harvesting, and processing steps involved in its creation.

1 Introduction

This paper provides an overview of the *PAISÀ* corpus of Italian web texts and an introductory description of the motivation, procedures and facilities for its creation and delivery.

Developed within the *PAISÀ* project, the corpus is intended to meet the objective to help overcome the technological barriers that still prevent web users from making use of large quantities of contemporary Italian texts for language and cultural education, by creating a comprehensive and easily accessible corpus resource of Italian.

The initial motivation of the initiative stemmed from the awareness that any static repertoire of digital data, however carefully designed and developed, is doomed to fast obsolescence, if contents are not freely available for public usage, continuously updated and checked for quality, incrementally augmented with new texts and annotation metadata for intelligent indexing and browsing. These requirements brought us to design a resource that was (1) freely available and freely re-publishable, (2) comprehensively covering contemporary common language and cultural content and (3) enhanced with a rich set of automatically-annotated linguistic information to enable advanced querying and retrieving of data. On top of that, we set out to develop (4) a dedicated interface with a low entry barrier for different target groups. The end result of this original plan represents an unprecedented digital language resource in the Italian scenario.

The main novelty of the *PAISÀ* web corpus is that it exclusively draws on Creative Commons licensed data, provides advanced linguistic annotations with respect to corpora of comparable size and corpora of web data, and invests in a carefully designed query interface, targeted at different user groups. In particular, the integration of richly annotated language content with an easily accessible, user-oriented interface makes *PAISÀ* a unique and flexible resource for language teaching.

2 Related Work

The world wide web, with its inexhaustible amount of natural language data, has become an established source for efficiently building large corpora (Kilgarriff and Grefenstette, 2003). Tools are available that make it convenient to bootstrap corpora from the web based on mere seed term lists, such as the BootCaT toolkit (Baroni and Bernardini, 2004). The huge corpora created by the WaCky project (Baroni et al., 2009) are an example of such an approach.

A large number of papers have recently been published on the harvesting, cleaning and processing of web corpora.[1] However, *freely available, large, contemporary, linguistically annotated, easily accessible* web corpora are still missing for many languages; but cf. e.g. (Généreux et al., 2012) and the Common Crawl Foundations (CCF) web crawl[2].

*EURAC Research Bolzano/Bozen, IT

†University of Bologna, IT

‡University of Leeds, UK

§ Institute of Computational Linguistics "Antonio Zampolli" - CNR, IT

¶Institut Jules Bordet, BE

||University of Pisa, IT

[1]cf. the Special Interest Group of the Association for Computational Linguistics on Web as Corpus (SIGWAC) http://sigwac.org.uk/

[2]CCF produces and maintains a repository of web crawl data that is openly accessible: http://commoncrawl.org/

3 Corpus Composition

3.1 Corpus design

PAISÀ aimed at creating a comprehensive corpus resource of Italian web texts which adheres to the criteria laid out in section 1. For these criteria to be fully met, we had to address a wide variety of issues covering the entire life-cycle of a digital text resource, ranging from robust algorithms for web navigation and harvesting, to adaptive annotation tools for advanced text indexing and querying and user-friendly accessing and rendering online interfaces customisable for different target groups.

Initially, we targeted a size of 100M tokens, and planned to automatically annotate the data with lemma, part-of-speech, structural dependency, and advanced linguistic information, using and adapting standard annotation tools (cf. section 4). Integration into a querying environment and a dedicated online interface were planned.

3.2 Licenses

A crucial point when planning to compile a corpus that is free to redistribute without encountering legal copyright issues is to collect texts that are in the public domain or at least, have been made available in a copyleft regime. This is the case when the author of a certain document decided to share some rights (copy and/or distribute, adapt etc.) on her work with the public, in a way that end users do not need to ask permission to the creator/owner of the original work. This is possible by employing licenses other than the traditional "all right reserved" copyright, i.e. GNU, Creative Commons etc., which found a wide use especially on the web. Exploratory studies (Brunello, 2009) have shown that Creative Commons licenses are widely employed throughout the web (at least on the Italian webspace), enough to consider the possibility to build a large corpus from the web exclusively made of documents released under such licenses.

In particular, Creative Commons provides five basic "baseline rights": *Attribution (BY), Share Alike (SA), Non Commercial (NC), No Derivative Works (ND)*. The licenses themselves are composed of at least *Attribution* (which can be used even alone) plus the other elements, allowing six different combinations:[3] (1) Attribution (CC BY), (2) Attribution-NonCommercial (CC BY-NC), (3) Attribution-ShareAlike (CC BY-SA), (4) Attribution-NoDerivs (CC BY-ND), (5) Attribution-NonCommercial-ShareAlike (CC BY-NC-SA), and (6) Attribution-NonCommercial-NoDerivs (CC BY-NC-ND).

Some combinations are not possible because certain elements are not compatible, e.g. *Share Alike* and *No Derivative Works*. For our purposes we decided to discard documents released with the two licenses containing the *No Derivative Works* option, because our corpus is in fact a derivative work of collected documents.

3.3 The final corpus

The corpus contains approximately 388,000 documents from 1,067 different websites, for a total of about 250M tokens. All documents contained in the *PAISÀ* corpus date back to Sept./Oct. 2010.

The documents come from several web sources which, at the time of corpus collection, provided their content under Creative Commons license (see section 3.2 for details). About 269,000 texts are from Wikimedia Foundation projects, with approximately 263,300 pages from Wikipedia, 2380 pages from Wikibooks, 1680 pages from Wikinews, 740 pages from Wikiversity, 410 pages from Wikisource, and 390 Wikivoyage pages.

The remaining 119,000 documents come from `guide.supereva.it` (ca. 19,000), `italy.indymedia.org` (ca. 10,000) and several blog services from more than another 1,000 different sites (e.g. `www.tvblog.it` (9,088 pages), `www.motoblog.it` (3,300), `www.ecowebnews.it` (3,220), and `www.webmasterpoint.org` (3,138).

Texts included in *PAISÀ* have an average length of 683 words, with the longest text[4] counting 66,380 running tokens. A non exhaustive list of average text lengths by source type is provided in table 1 by way of illustration.

The corpus has been annotated for lemma, part-of-speech and dependency information (see section 4.2 for details). At the document level, the corpus contains information on the URL of origin and a set of descriptive statistics of the text, including text length, rate of advanced vocabulary, readability parameters, etc. (see section 4.3). Also, each document is marked with a unique identifier.

[3]For detailed descriptions of each license see `http://creativecommons.org/licenses/`

[4]The *European Constitution* from wikisource.org: `http://it.wikisource.org/wiki/Trattato_che_adotta_una_Costituzione_per_l'Europa`

Document source	Avg text length
PAISÀ total	683 words
Wikipedia	693 words
Wikibooks	1844 words
guide.supereva.it	378 words
italy.indymedia.it	1147 words
tvblog.it	1472 words
motoblog.it	421 words
ecowebnews.it	347 words
webmasterpoint.org	332 words

Table 1: Average text length by source

The annotated corpus adheres to the standard CoNLL column-based format (Buchholz and Marsi, 2006), is encoded in UTF-8.

4 Corpus Creation

4.1 Collecting and cleaning web data

The web pages for *PAISÀ* were selected in two ways: part of the corpus collection was made through CC-focused web crawling, and another part through a targeted collection of documents from specific websites.

4.1.1 Seed-term based harvesting

At the time of corpus collection (2010), we used the BootCaT toolkit mainly because collecting URLs could be based on the public Yahoo! search API[5], including the option to restrict search to CC-licensed pages (including the possibility to specify even the particular licenses). Unfortunately, Yahoo! discontinued the free availability of this API, and BootCaT's remaining search engines do not provide this feature.

An earlier version of the corpus was collected using the tuple list originally employed to build itWaC[6]. As we noticed that the use of this list, in combination with the restriction to CC, biased the final results (i.e. specific websites occurred very often as top results) , we provided as input 50,000 medium frequent seed terms from a basic Italian vocabulary list[7], in order to get a wider distribution of search queries, and, ultimately, of texts.

As introduced in section 3.2, we restricted the selection not just to Creative Commons-licensed texts, but specifically to those licenses allowing redistribution: namely, CC BY, CC BY-SA, CC BY-NC-SA, and CC BY-NC.

Results were downloaded and automatically cleaned with the KrdWrd system, an environment for the unified processing of web content (Steger and Stemle, 2009).

Wrongly CC-tagged pages were eliminated using a black-list that had been manually populated following inspection of earlier corpus versions.

4.1.2 Targeted

In September 2009, the Wikimedia Foundation decided to release the content of their wikis under CC BY-SA[8], so we decided to download the large and varied amount of texts made available through the Italian versions of these websites. This was done using the Wikipedia Extractor[9] on official dumps[10] of Wikipedia, Wikinews, Wikisource, Wikibooks, Wikiversity and Wikivoyage.

4.2 Linguistic annotation and tools adaptation

The corpus was automatically annotated with lemma, part-of-speech and dependency information, using state-of-the-art annotation tools for Italian. Part-of-speech tagging was performed with the Part-Of-Speech tagger described in Dell'Orletta (2009) and dependency-parsed by the DeSR parser (Attardi et al., 2009), using *Multilayer Perceptron* as the learning algorithm. The systems used the ISST-TANL part-of-speech[11] and dependency tagsets[12]. In particular, the pos-tagger achieves a performance of 96.34% and DeSR, trained on the ISST-TANL treebank consisting of articles from newspapers and periodicals, achieves a performance of 83.38% and 87.71% in terms of LAS (*labelled attachment score*) and UAS (*unlabelled attachment score*) respectively, when tested on texts of the same type.

However, since Gildea (2001), it is widely acknowledged that statistical NLP tools have a drop of accuracy when tested against corpora differing from the typology of texts on which they were trained. This also holds true for *PAISÀ*: it contains

[5] http://developer.yahoo.com/boss/

[6] http://wacky.sslmit.unibo.it/doku.php?id=seed_words_and_tuples

[7] http://ppbm.paravia.it/dib_lemmario.php

[8] Previously under GNU Free Documentation License.

[9] http://medialab.di.unipi.it/wiki/Wikipedia_Extractor

[10] http://dumps.wikimedia.org/

[11] http://www.italianlp.it/docs/ISST-TANL-POStagset.pdf

[12] http://www.italianlp.it/docs/ISST-TANL-DEPtagset.pdf

lexical and syntactic structures of non-canonical languages such as the language of social media, blogs, forum posts, consumer reviews, etc. As reported in Petrov and McDonald (2012), there are multiple reasons why parsing the web texts is difficult: punctuation and capitalization are often inconsistent, there is a lexical shift due to increased use of slang and technical jargon, some syntactic constructions are more frequent in web text than in newswire, etc.

In order to overcome this problem, two main typologies of methods and techniques have been developed: *Self-training* (McClosky et al., 2006) and *Active Learning* (Thompson et al., 1999).

For the specific purpose of the NLP tools adaptation to the Italian web texts, we adopted two different strategies for the pos-tagger and the parser. For what concerns pos-tagging, we used an active learning approach: given a subset of automatically pos-tagged sentences of *PAISÀ*, we selected the ones with the lowest likelihood, where the sentence likelihood was computed as the product of the probabilities of the assignments of the pos-tagger for all the tokens. These sentences were manually revised and added to the training corpus in order to build a new pos-tagger model incorporating some new knowledge from the target domain.

For what concerns parsing, we used a self-training approach to domain adaptation described in Dell'Orletta et al. (2013), based on ULISSE (Dell'Orletta et al., 2011). ULISSE is an unsupervised linguistically-driven algorithm to select reliable parses from a collection of dependency annotated texts. It assigns to each dependency tree a score quantifying its reliability based on a wide range of linguistic features. After collecting statistics about selected features from a corpus of automatically parsed sentences, for each newly parsed sentence ULISSE computes a reliability score using the previously extracted feature statistics. From the top of the parses (ranked according to their reliability score) different pools of parses were selected to be used for training. The new training contains the original training set as well as the new selected parses which include lexical and syntactic characteristics specific of the target domain (Italian web texts). The parser trained on this new training set improves its performance when tested on the target domain.

We used this domain adaptation approach for the following three main reasons: a) it is unsupervised (i.e. no need for manually annotated training data); b) unlike the *Active Learning* approach used for pos-tagging, it does not need manual revision of the automatically parsed samples to be used for training; c) it was previously tested on Italian texts with good results (Dell'Orletta et al., 2013).

4.3 Readability analysis of corpus documents

For each corpus document, we calculated several text statistics indicative of the linguistic complexity, or 'readability' of a text.

The applied measures include, (1) *text length in tokens*, that is the number of tokens per text, (2) *sentences per text*, that is a sentence count, and (3) *type-token ratio* indicated as a percentage value. In addition, we calculated (4) the *advanced vocabulary per text*, that is a word count of the text vocabulary which is not part of the the basic Italian vocabulary ('vocabolario di base') for written texts, as defined by De Mauro (1991)[13], and (5) the *Gulpease Index* ('Indice Gulpease') (Lucisano and Piemontese, 1988), which is a measure for the readability of text that is based on frequency relations between the number of sentences, words and letters of a text.

All values are encoded as metadata for the corpus. Via the *PAISÀ* online interface, they can be employed for filtering documents and building subcorpora. This facility was implemented with the principal target group of *PAISÀ* users in mind, as the selection of language examples according to their readability level is particularly relevant for language learning and teaching.

4.4 Attempts at text classification for genre, topic, and function

Lack of information about the composition of corpora collected from the web using unsupervised methods is probably one of the major limitations of current web corpora vis-à-vis more traditional, carefully constructed corpora, most notably when applications to language teaching and learning are envisaged. This also holds true for *PAISÀ*, es-

[13]The advanced vocabulary was calculated on the basis of a word list consisting of De Mauro's 'vocabolario fondamentale' (`http://it.wikipedia.org/wiki/Vocabolario_fondamentale`) and 'vocabolario di alto uso' (`http://it.wikipedia.org/wiki/Vocabolario_di_alto_uso`), together with high frequent function words not contained in those two lists.

pecially for the harvested[14] subcorpus that was downloaded as described in section 4.1. We therefore carried out some experiments with the ultimate aim to enrich the corpus with metadata about text genre, topic and function, using automated techniques.

In order to gain some insights into the composition of *PAISÀ*, we first conducted some manual investigations. Drawing on existing literature on web genres (e.g. (Santini, 2005; Rehm et al., 2008; Santini et al., 2010)) and text classification according to text function and topic (e.g. (Sharoff, 2006)), we developed a tentative three-fold taxonomy to be used for text classification. Following four cycles of sample manual annotation by three annotators, categories were adjusted in order to better reflect the nature of *PAISÀ*'s web documents (cf. (Sharoff, 2010) about differences between domains covered in the BNC and in the web-derived ukWaC). Details about the taxonomy are provided in Borghetti et al. (2011). Then, we started to cross-check whether the devised taxonomy was indeed appropriate to describe *PAISÀ*'s composition by comparing its categories with data resulting from the application of unsupervised methods for text classification.

Interesting insights have emerged so far regarding the topic category. Following Sharoff (2010), we used topic modelling based on *Latent Dirichlet Allocation* for the detection of topics: 20 clusters/topics were identified on the basis of keywords (the number of clusters to retrieve is a user-defined parameter) and projected onto the manually defined taxonomy. This revealed that most of the 20 automatically identified topics could be reasonably matched to one of the 8 categories included in the taxonomy; exceptions were represented by clusters characterised by proper nouns and general language words such *bambino/uomo/famiglia* ('child'/'man'/'family') or *credere/sentire/sperare* ('to believe'/'feel'/'hope'), which may in fact be indicative of genres such as diary or personal comment (e.g. personal blog). Only one of the categories originally included in the taxonomy – natural sciences – was not represented in the clusters, which may indicate that there are few texts within *PAISÀ* belonging to this domain. One of the major advantages of topic models is that each corpus document can be associated – to varying degrees – to several topics/clusters: if encoded as metadata, this information makes it possible not only to filter texts according to their prevailing domain, but also to represent the heterogeneous nature of many web documents.

[14]In fact, even the nature of the targeted texts is not precisely defined: for instance, Wikipedia articles can actually encompass a variety of text types such as biographies, introductions to academic theories etc. (Santini et al., 2010, p. 15)

5 Corpus Access and Usage

5.1 Corpus distribution

The *PAISÀ* corpus is distributed in two ways: it is made available for download and it can be queried via its online interface. For both cases, no restrictions on its usage apply other than those defined by the Creative Commons BY-NC-SA license. For corpus download, both the raw text version and the annotated corpus in CoNLL format are provided.

The *PAISÀ* corpus together with all project-related information is accessible via the project web site at `http://www.corpusitaliano.it`

5.2 Corpus interface

The creation of a dedicated open online interface for the *PAISÀ* corpus has been a declared primary objective of the project.

The interface is aimed at providing a powerful, effective and easy-to-employ tool for making full use of the resource, without having to go through downloading, installation or registration procedures. It is targeted at different user groups, particularly language learners, teachers, and linguists. As users of *PAISÀ* are expected to show varying levels of proficiency in terms of language competence, linguistic knowledge, and concerning the use of online search tools, the interface has been designed to provide four separate search components, implementing different query modes.

Initially, the user is directed to a basic keyword search that adopts a 'Google-style' search box. Single search terms, as well as multi-word combinations or sequences can be searched by inserting them in a simple text box.

The second component is an advanced graphical search form. It provides elaborated search options for querying linguistic annotation layers and allows for defining distances between search terms as well as repetitions or optionally occurring terms. Furthermore, the advanced search supports regular expressions.

The third component emulates a command-line search via the powerful CQP query language of the Open Corpus Workbench (Evert and Hardie, 2011). It allows for complex search queries in CQP syntax that rely on linguistic annotation layers as well as on metadata information.

Finally, a filter interface is presented in a fourth component. It serves the purpose of retrieving full-text corpus documents based on keyword searches as well as text statistics (see section 4.3). Like the CQP interface, the filter interface is also supporting the building of temporary subcorpora for subsequent querying.

By default, search results are displayed as KWIC (KeyWord In Context) lines, centred around the search expression. Each search hit can be expanded to its full sentence view. In addition, the originating full text document can be accessed and its source URL is provided.

Based on an interactive visualisation for dependency graphs (Culy et al., 2011) for each search result a graphical representations of dependency relations together with the sentence and associated lemma and part-of-speech information can be generated (see Figure 1).

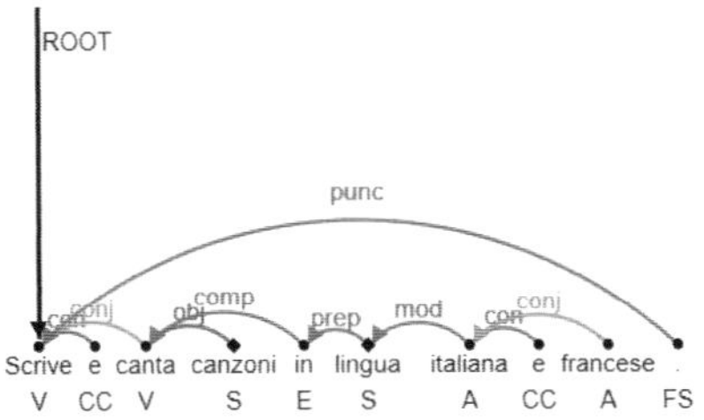

Figure 1: Dependency diagram

Targeted at novice language learners of Italian, a filter for automatically restricting search results to sentences of limited complexity has been integrated into each search component. When activated, search results are automatically filtered based on a combination of the complexity measures introduced in section 4.3.

5.3 Technical details

The *PAISÀ* online interface has been developed in several layers: in essence, it provides a front-end to the corpus as indexed in Open Corpus Workbench (Evert and Hardie, 2011). This corpus query engine provides the fundamental search capabilities through the CQP language. Based on the CWB/Perl API that is part of the Open Corpus Workbench package, a web service has been developed at EURAC which exposes a large part of the CQP language[15] through a RESTful API.[16]

The four types of searches provided by the online interface are developed on top of this web service. The user queries are translated into CQP queries and passed to the web service. In many cases, such as the free word order queries in the simple and advanced search forms, more than one CQP query is necessary to produce the desired result. Other functionalities implemented in this layer are the management of subcorpora and the filtering by complexity. The results returned by the web service are then formatted and presented to the user.

The user interface as well as the mechanisms for translation of queries from the web forms into CQP have been developed server-side in PHP. The visualizations are implemented client-side in JavaScript and jQuery, the dependency graphs based on the xLDD framework (Culy et al., 2011).

5.4 Extraction of lexico-syntactic information

PAISÀ is currently used in the CombiNet project "Word Combinations in Italian – Theoretical and descriptive analysis, computational models, lexicographic layout and creation of a dictionary".[17] The project goal is to study the combinatory properties of Italian words by developing advanced computational linguistics methods for extracting distributional information from *PAISÀ*.

In particular, CombiNet uses a pattern-based approach to extract a wide range of multiword expressions, such as phrasal lexemes, collocations, and usual combinations. POS n-grams are automatically extracted from *PAISÀ*, and then ranked according to different types of association measures (e.g., pointwise mutual information, log-likelihood ratios, etc.). Extending the LexIt methodology (Lenci et al., 2012), CombiNet also extracts distributional profiles from the parsed layer of *PAISÀ*, including the following types of information:

1. syntactic slots (subject, complements, modi-

[15] To safeguard the system against malicious attacks, security measures had to be taken at several of the layers, which unfortunately also make some of the more advanced CQP features inaccessible to the user.

[16] Web services based on REST (Representational State Transfer) principles employ standard concepts such as a URI and standard HTTP methods to provide an interface to functionalities on a remote host.

[17] 3-year PRIN(2010/2011)-project, coordination by Raffaele Simone – University of Rome Tre

fiers, etc.) and subcategorization frames;

2. lexical sets filling syntactic slots (e.g. prototypical subjects of a target verb);

3. semantic classes describing selectional preferences of syntactic slots (e.g. the direct obj. of *mangiare*/'to eat' typically selects nouns referring to food, while its subject selects animate nouns); semantic roles of predicates.

The saliency and typicality of combinatory patterns are weighted by means of different statistical indexes and the resulting profiles will be used to define a distributional semantic classification of Italian verbs, comparable to the one elaborated in the VerbNet project (Kipper et al., 2008).

6 Evaluation

We performed post-crawl evaluations on the data. For licensing, we analysed 200,534 pages that were originally collected for the *PAISÀ* corpus, and only 1,060 were identified as containing no CC license link (99.95% with CC mark-up). Then, from 10,000 randomly selected non-CC-licensed Italian pages 15 were wrongly identified as CC licensed containing CC mark-up (0.15% error). For language identification we checked the harvested corpus part with the CLD2 toolkit[18], and $> 99\%$ of the data was identified as Italian.

The pos-tagger has been adapted to peculiarities of the *PAISÀ* web texts, by manually correcting sample annotation output and re-training the tagger accordingly. Following the active learning approach as described in section 4.2 we built a new pos-tagger model based on 40.000 manually revised tokens. With the new model, we obtained an improvement in accuracy of 1% on a test-set of 5000 tokens extracted from *PAISÀ*. Final tagger accuracy reached 96.03%.

7 Conclusion / Future Work

In this paper we showed how a contemporary and free language resource of Italian with linguistic annotations can be designed, implemented and developed from the web and made available for different types of language users.

Future work will focus on enriching the corpus with metadata by means of automatic classification techniques, so as to make a better assessment of corpus composition. A multi-faceted approach combining linguistic features extracted from texts (content/function words ratio, sentence length, word frequency, etc.) and information extracted from document URLs (e.g., tags like "wiki", "blog") might be particularly suitable for genre and function annotation.

Metadata annotation will enable more advanced applications of the corpus for language teaching and learning purposes. In this respect, existing exemplifications of the use of the *PAISÀ* interface for language learning and teaching (Lyding et al., 2013) could be followed by further pedagogical proposals as well as empowered by dedicated teaching guidelines for the exploitation of the corpus and its web interface in the class of Italian as a second language.

In a more general perspective, we envisage a tighter integration between acquisition of new texts, automated text annotation and development of lexical and language learning resources allowing even non-specialised users to carve out and develop their own language data. This ambitious goal points in the direction of a fully-automatised control of the entire life-cycle of open-access Italian language resources with a view to address an increasingly wider range of potential demands.

Acknowledgements

The three years *PAISÀ* project[19], concluded in January 2013, received funding from the Italian Ministry of Education, Universities and Research (MIUR)[20], by the FIRB program (Fondo per gli Investimenti della Ricerca di Base)[21].

References

G. Attardi, F. Dell'Orletta, M. Simi, and J. Turian. 2009. Accurate dependency parsing with a stacked multilayer perceptron. In *Proc. of Evalita'09, Evaluation of NLP and Speech Tools for Italian*, Reggio Emilia.

M. Baroni and S. Bernardini. 2004. Bootcat: Bootstrapping corpora and terms from the web. In *Proc. of LREC 2004*, pages 1313–1316. ELDA.

M. Baroni, S. Bernardini, A. Ferraresi, and E. Zanchetta. 2009. The wacky wide web: A collection of very large linguistically processed

[18] Compact Language Detection 2, `http://code.google.com/p/cld2/`

[19] An effort of four Italian research units: University of Bologna, CNR Pisa, University of Trento and European Academy of Bolzano/Bozen.

[20] `http://www.istruzione.it/`

[21] `http://hubmiur.pubblica.istruzione.it/web/ricerca/firb`

web-crawled corpora. *Journal of LRE*, 43(3):209–226.

C. Borghetti, S. Castagnoli, and M. Brunello. 2011. I testi del web: una proposta di classificazione sulla base del corpus paisà. In M. Cerruti, E. Corino, and C. Onesti, editors, *Formale e informale. La variazione di registro nella comunicazione elettronica.*, pages 147–170. Carocci, Roma.

M. Brunello. 2009. The creation of free linguistic corpora from the web. In I. Alegria, I. Leturia, and S. Sharoff, editors, *Proc. of the Fifth Web as Corpus Workshop (WAC5)*, pages 9–16. Elhuyar Fundazioa.

S. Buchholz and E. Marsi. 2006. CoNLL-X Shared Task on Multilingual Dependency Parsing. In *Proc. Tenth Conf. Comput. Nat. Lang. Learn.*, number June in CoNLL-X '06, pages 149–164. Association for Computational Linguistics.

C. Culy, V. Lyding, and H. Dittmann. 2011. xldd: Extended linguistic dependency diagrams. In *Proc. of the 15th International Conference on Information Visualisation IV2011*, pages 164–169, London, UK.

T. De Mauro. 1991. *Guida all'uso delle parole.* Editori Riuniti, Roma.

F. Dell'Orletta, G. Venturi, and S. Montemagni. 2011. Ulisse: an unsupervised algorithm for detecting reliable dependency parses. In *Proc. of CoNLL 2011, Conferences on Natural Language Learning*, Portland, Oregon.

F. Dell'Orletta, G. Venturi, and S. Montemagni. 2013. Unsupervised linguistically-driven reliable dependency parses detection and self-training for adaptation to the biomedical domain. In *Proc. of BioNLP 2013, Workshop on Biomedical NLP*, Sofia.

F. Dell'Orletta. 2009. Ensemble system for part-of-speech tagging. In *Proceedings of Evalita'09, Evaluation of NLP and Speech Tools for Italian*, Reggio Emilia.

S. Evert and A. Hardie. 2011. Twenty-first century corpus workbench: Updating a query architecture for the new millennium. In *Proc. of the Corpus Linguistics 2011*, Birmingham, UK.

M. Généreux, I. Hendrickx, and A. Mendes. 2012. A large portuguese corpus on-line: Cleaning and preprocessing. In *PROPOR*, volume 7243 of *Lecture Notes in Computer Science*, pages 113–120. Springer.

A. Kilgarriff and G. Grefenstette. 2003. Introduction to the special issue on the web as corpus. *Computational Linguistics*, 29(3):333–347.

K. Kipper, A. Korhonen, N. Ryant, and M. Palmer. 2008. A large-scale classification of english verbs. *Journal of LRE*, 42:21–40.

A. Lenci, G. Lapesa, and G. Bonansinga. 2012. Lexit: A computational resource on italian argument structure. In N. Calzolari, K. Choukri, T. Declerck, M. Uğur Doğan, B. Maegaard, J. Mariani, J. Odijk, and S. Piperidis, editors, *Proc. of LREC 2012*, pages 3712–3718, Istanbul, Turkey, May. ELRA.

P. Lucisano and M. E. Piemontese. 1988. Gulpease: una formula per la predizione della difficolt dei testi in lingua italiana. *Scuola e città*, 39(3):110–124.

V. Lyding, C. Borghetti, H. Dittmann, L. Nicolas, and E. Stemle. 2013. Open corpus interface for italian language learning. In *Proc. of the ICT for Language Learning Conference, 6th Edition*, Florence, Italy.

D. McClosky, E. Charniak, and M. Johnson. 2006. Reranking and self-training for parser adaptation. In *Proc. of ACL 2006, ACL*, Sydney.

S. Petrov and R. McDonald. 2012. Overview of the 2012 shared task on parsing the web. In *Proc. of SANCL 2012, First Workshop on Syntactic Analysis of Non-Canonical Language*, Montreal.

G. Rehm, M. Santini, A. Mehler, P. Braslavski, R. Gleim, A. Stubbe, S. Symonenko, M. Tavosanis, and V. Vidulin. 2008. Towards a reference corpus of web genres for the evaluation of genre identification systems. In *Proc. of LREC 2008*, pages 351–358, Marrakech, Morocco.

M. Santini, A. Mehler, and S. Sharoff. 2010. Riding the Rough Waves of Genre on the Web. Concepts and Research Questions. In A. Mehler, S. Sharoff, and M. Santini, editors, *Genres on the Web: Computational Models and Empirical Studies.*, pages 3–33. Springer, Dordrecht.

M. Santini. 2005. Genres in formation? an exploratory study of web pages using cluster analysis. In *Proc. of the 8th Annual Colloquium for the UK Special Interest Group for Computational Linguistics (CLUK05)*, Manchester, UK.

S. Sharoff. 2006. Creating General-Purpose Corpora Using Automated Search Engine Queries. In M. Baroni and S. Bernardini, editors, *Wacky! Working Papers on the Web as Corpus*, pages 63–98. Gedit, Bologna.

S. Sharoff. 2010. Analysing similarities and differences between corpora. In *7th Language Technologies Conference*, Ljubljana.

J. M. Steger and E. W. Stemle. 2009. KrdWrd – The Architecture for Unified Processing of Web Content. In *Proc. Fifth Web as Corpus Work.*, Donostia-San Sebastian, Basque Country.

C. A. Thompson, M. E. Califf, and R. J. Mooney. 1999. Active learning for natural language parsing and information extraction. In *Proc. of ICML99, the Sixteenth International Conference on Machine Learning*, San Francisco, CA.

Author Index